Culture and Customs of Angola

Angola. Cartography by Bookcomp, Inc.

Culture and Customs of Angola

∽⚬∽

ADEBAYO O. OYEBADE

Culture and Customs of Africa
Toyin Falola, Series Editor

GREENWOOD PRESS
Westport, Connecticut • London

Library of Congress Cataloging-in-Publication Data

Oyebade, Adebayo.
  Culture and customs of Angola / Adebayo O. Oyebade.
    p. cm.—(Culture and customs of Africa, ISSN 1530–8367)
  Includes bibliographical references and index.
  ISBN 0–313–33147–2 (alk. paper)
  1. Angola—Civilization. 2. Angola—Social life and customs. 3. Angola—Intellectual life. I. Title.
  DT1302.O94 2007
  967.3—dc22   2006028864

British Library Cataloguing in Publication Data is available.

Library of Congress Catalog Card Number: 2006028864
ISBN-10: 0–313–33147–2
ISBN-13: 978–313–33147–3
ISSN: 1530–8367

First published in 2007

Greenwood Press, 88 Post Road West, Westport, CT 06881
An imprint of Greenwood Publishing Group, Inc.
www.greenwood.com

Printed in the United States of America

The paper used in this book complies with the
Permanent Paper Standard issued by the National
Information Standards Organization (Z39.48–1984).

10 9 8 7 6 5 4 3 2 1

Contents

Series Foreword

AFRICA IS A VAST continent, the second largest, after Asia. It is four times the size of the United States, excluding Alaska. It is the cradle of human civilization. A diverse continent, Africa has more than fifty countries with a population of over 700 million people who speak over 1,000 languages. Ecological and cultural differences vary from one region to another. As an old continent, Africa is one of the richest in culture and customs, and its contributions to world civilization are impressive indeed.

Africans regard culture as essential to their lives and future development. Culture embodies their philosophy, worldview, behavior patterns, arts, and institutions. The books in this series intend to capture the comprehensiveness of African culture and customs, dwelling on such important aspects as religion, worldview, literature, media, art, housing, architecture, cuisine, traditional dress, gender, marriage, family, lifestyles, social customs, music, and dance.

The uses and definitions of "culture" vary, reflecting its prestigious association with civilization and social status, its restriction to attitude and behavior, its globalization, and the debates surrounding issues of tradition, modernity, and postmodernity. The participating authors have chosen a comprehensive meaning of culture while not ignoring the alternative uses of the term.

Each volume in the series focuses on a single country, and the format is uniform. The first chapter presents a historical overview, in addition to information on geography, economy, and politics. Each volume then proceeds to examine the various aspects of culture and customs. The series highlights the mechanisms for the transmission of tradition and culture across generations: the significance of orality, traditions, kinship rites, and family property

distribution; the rise of print culture; and the impact of educational institutions. The series also explores the intersections between local, regional,
national, and global bases for identity and social relations. While the volumes
are organized nationally, they pay attention to ethnicity and language groups
and the links between Africa and the wider world.

The books in the series capture the elements of continuity and change
in culture and customs. Custom is represented not as static or as a museum
artifact but as a dynamic phenomenon. Furthermore, the authors recognize
the current challenges to traditional wisdom, which include gender relations,
the negotiation of local identities in relation to the state, the significance of
struggles for power at national and local levels and their impact on cultural
traditions and community-based forms of authority, and the tensions
between agrarian and industrial/manufacturing/oil-based economic modes
of production.

Africa is a continent of great changes, instigated mainly by Africans but
also through influences from other continents. The rise of youth culture, the
penetration of the global media, and the challenges to generational stability
are some of the components of modern changes explored in the series. The
ways in which traditional (non-Western and nonimitative) African cultural
forms continue to survive and thrive—that is, how they have taken advan-
tage of the market system to enhance their influence and reproductions—also
receive attention.

Through the books in this series, readers can see their own cultures in a different perspective, understand the habits of Africans, and educate themselves
about the customs and cultures of other countries and people. The hope is
that the readers will come to respect the cultures of others and see them not
as inferior or superior to theirs but merely as different. Africa has always been
important to Europe and the United States, essentially as a source of labor,
raw materials, and markets. Blacks are in Europe and the Americas as part
of the African diaspora, a migration that took place primarily because of the
slave trade. Recent African migrants increasingly swell their number and vis-
ibility. It is important to understand the history of the diaspora and the newer
migrants as well as the roots of the culture and customs of the places from
where they come. It is equally important to understand others in order to be
able to interact successfully in a world that keeps shrinking. The accessible
nature of the books in this series will contribute to this understanding and
enhance the quality of human interaction in a new millennium.

Toyin Falola
Frances Higginbothom, Nalle Centennial Professor in History
The University of Texas at Austin

Chronology

Pre-seventh century	A number of Khoisan hunter-gatherer groups inhabit regions of present-day Angola. They do not evolve centralized states or complex political systems, and their economy is based mainly on hunting wild animals and gathering wild fruits.
1200s	Arrival to the Angolan region of the so-called Bantu from the area around Nigeria and Cameroon.
1300s	The rise of the Kingdom of Kongo, the most enterprising precolonial state in Southwest Africa, of which northern Angola is part.
1483	The Portuguese arrive in the region of present-day northern Angola.
1490	Portugal sends an ambassador, Gonçalo de Sousa, to establish an embassy in Angola. De Sousa is accompanied by the first missionaries to go to the region.
1500–1700s	Angola becomes a major slave-trading area for the Portuguese. The Angolan area feed parts of South America, especially Brazil and Cuba, with several million African slaves. Luanda is the major Portuguese slave-trading port in the late sixteenth century and for most of the seventeenth century. It is joined by Benguela in the 1600s and remains an important slave-trading port by the late eighteenth century.
1500–1850	An estimated four million people are transported from Angola to the New World.
1575	Sao Paulo de Loanda (Luanda) is founded.
1576	The Portuguese build a fort at Luanda.

1592	Luanda becomes a Portuguese's colony.
1617	Benguela is established.
1641	The Dutch take Luanda.
1648	The Portuguese recover Luanda.
1663	Death of the warrior queen Nzinga Mbande (known also as Jinga or Ginga) of the kingdom of Ndongo, who led her military force to oppose Portuguese imperialism.
1764–1850	The gradual transformation of Angola from a slave-trading society to a subsistence economy. By 1850, Luanda is a major commercial city along the southwestern coast of Africa boasting many commercial firms.
1836	Portugal officially abolishes the slave trade.
1849	Our Lord Jesus Christ Church in the World (Igreja do Nosso Senhor Jesus Cristo no Mundo) is established by Simon Mtoko (Simão Toco), a charismatic figure from Uíge Province.
1858	Slavery is abolished in Angola.
1878	The English Baptist church establishes the first Protestant mission in Angola at São Salvador (now M'banza Kongo).
1884	Portugal's claim to Angola is recognized by other European powers at the Berlin West African Conference.
1885–1930	Portugal consolidates colonial authority over Angola, even though local resistance continues.
1902	The collapse of Mbundu resistance to European imperialism.
1903	The collapse of Ovimbundu's resistance to European imperialism.
1912	Huambo is established by the Portuguese. It is called Nova Lisboa (New Lisbon) before 1975.
1914	Chokwe's resistance to European imperialism collapses.
1931	The Benguela railroad is completed.
1950s	The anticolonial movement gathers momentum, which inevitably leads to armed struggle in the early 1960s. Portugal's repression of colonial expression of nationalism leads to the emergence of underground revolutionary movements that start the guerrilla war against the colonial power.
1951	The status of Angola changes from colony to overseas province and comes under the authority of a governor-general.
1953	Establishment of the Party of the United Struggle for Africans in Angola (Partido da Luta Unida dos Africanos de Angola, PLUA), the earliest nationalist movement to demand independence.

1955	The Angolan Communist Party (Partido Comunista Angolano, PCA) is formed under the leadership of two brothers, Mário Pinto de Andrade and Joaquim Pinto de Andrade. The party is influenced by the Portuguese Communist Party.
1956	PLUA merges with the PCA to form the Popular Movement for the Liberation of Angola (Movimento Popular de Libertação de Angola, MPLA), one of the three major nationalist movements that fight for Angola's independence. It is established under the leadership of Antonio Agostinho Neto. Other nationalist movements such as the Movement for the National Independence of Angola (MINA) and the Democratic Front for the Liberation of Angola (FDLA) subsequently merge with the MPLA. After attaining independence in 1975, the MPLA becomes the ruling party and Neto becomes Angola's first president. The party adopts a Marxist-Leninist ideology, establishes a one-party socialist state, and maintains close ties with the Soviet Union and other Communist-bloc states. The MPLA has ruled Angola since independence and is presently under the leadership of José Eduardo dos Santos, who succeeded Neto in 1979 as Angola's president.
1959 May 25	President Nikita Khrushchev, leader of the Soviet Union, visits Angola.
1960s	Oil exploration commences, principally under foreign companies such as BP Amoco, ChevronTexaco, ExxonMobil, Shell, AGIP, and Total.
1961	The colonial government abolishes forced labor following deadly revolts on coffee plantations. The war of independence begins.
1962 March 15	The second of the major nationalist movements that fight the Portuguese for independence, the National Front for the Liberation of Angola (Frente Nacional de Libertação de Angola, FNLA), is established. Formed and led by Holden Roberto, the FNLA originally emerged in July 1957 as the Union of Peoples of Northern Angola (União das Populações do Norte de Angola, UPNA) to defend the interest of the Bakongo in the north. It becomes in 1958 the Union of Angolan Peoples (União das Populações de Angola, UPA), and in 1962, the FNLA, after merging with other northern groups. FNLA receives support from the United States and China. Although it continues to exist as a shell of its former self under various names, after 1988 it is no longer a political force in Angola.

August 21   The establishment of Agostinho Neto University (Universidade de Agostinho Neto, UAN) in Luanda, as a higher education institute.

1966

March 13   The third of the major nationalist movements that fight for independence, the National Union for the Total Independence of Angola (União Nacional para a Independência Total de Angola, UNITA), is established. This movement, headed by Jonas Savimbi, is backed by South Africa and, for a long time, the United States. It becomes a political party in 2002 at the end of the civil war.

1974

April 25   A military coup overthrows the dictatorship of Prime Minister Marcelo Caetano. The event leads to the collapse of the Portuguese colonial empire in Africa and thus paves the way for Angolan independence in 1975.

1975

January 15   The Alvir Agreement, which stipulates the formation of a transitional government in Angola as a precursor to independence, is signed between the new Lisbon government and the African nationalist movements: the MPLA, UNITA, and the FNLA.

January 31   A transitional government is inaugurated with a power-sharing arrangement between the nationalist movements. The political arrangement breaks down and the civil war begins with fighting between the MPLA and FNLA.

July   UNITA becomes involved in the civil war. The MPLA receives Cuban military support, FNLA is backed by Zaire (now known as Democratic Republic of Congo), and UNITA has U.S. military and financial support.

August   Troops of the South African Defence Force (SADF) enter Angola and occupy the Cunene region. Allied with UNITA forces, SADF begins a northward drive.

November 5   Cuban troops begin active fighting in Angola on MPLA side. Western sources estimate the number of Cuban soldiers at 2,000 by mid-November and 14,000 by February 1976.

November 11   Portugal formally grants independence to Angola after 14 years of guerrilla war. Amid the escalating war, the MPLA in control in the capital, Luanda, proclaim the People's Republic of Angola.

1976

January   The MPLA is on the offensive in the civil war due to massive Soviet supply of materials. By November it has achieved an upper hand against UNITA-SADF and FNLA.

February 11	Angola is recognized by the Organization of African Unity (OAU) as a member state. It also becomes a full member of the United Nations (UN) on December 1, following a unanimous vote of the Security Council.
February 22	The government of Portugal recognizes the MPLA government.
June 9	Sociedade Nacional de Combustiveis de Angola (Sonangol), a state-owned corporation, is established to oversee the management of the oil sector.

1977

September	The Union of Churches of the Holy Spirit in Angola (UIESA) holds a thanksgiving service in Luanda and in other places to demand for peace.
December	The Roman Catholic Church publicly accuses the government of violation of freedom of religion.
	At its congress, MPLA becomes MPLA-PT after adding to its name Party of Labor (Partido do Trabalho, PT). MPLA also formally adopts Marxism-Leninism as party and state ideology.

1978

May 4	Apartheid South African forces launch major attack on South West African People's Organization (SWAPO) bases inside Angola. UN Security Council condemns the attack on May 6.

1979

September 10	Agostinho Neto, Angola's first president and MPLA leader, dies. He is succeeded as president by José Eduardo dos Santos.

1984 | FNLA drops out of the civil war. |

1988 | South Africa and Cuba sign an agreement of mutual withdrawal from Angola. The war continues between the MPLA and UNITA. |

1989

January	Cuba begins to withdraw its 50,000 troops from Angola.
June	President José Eduardo dos Santos and UNITA leader Jonas Savimbi agree to a cease-fire after 14 years of civil war. The cease-fire does not hold, and the war continues.
November	Roman Catholic bishops call on UNITA and the MPLA to end the civil war and hold free elections.

1991

April	The MPLA formally renounces Marxism as state ideology.
May 24	Cuba completes the withdrawal of its remaining troops in Angola.

May 31	In Lisbon, President José Eduardo dos Santos and Jonas Savimbi sign the Bicesse Accord, a peace treaty that leads to the first elections, which are held in 1992.

1992

August	The name People's Republic of Angola is dropped, and the nation becomes known as the Republic of Angola. The MPLA earlier dropped its Marxist-Leninist ideology in favor of social democracy.
September 29, 30	The first multiparty elections in Angola are held and certified free and fair by UN observers. MPLA wins with absolute majority, and José Eduardo dos Santos is elected president. UNITA and its leader, Jonas Savimbi, reject the election results. The civil war resumes.

1993

March	Huambo is captured by UNITA forces. The siege of the rebel forces leads to extensive damage to the city, heavy civilian casualties, and massive population displacement.
September 15	The UN imposes an arms and oil embargo against UNITA.

1994

November 20	In Zambia, President José Eduardo dos Santos and Savimbi, leader of UNITA, sign the Lusaka Protocol, which calls for an end to the war and requires UNITA to demobilize its 70,000-member army. UNITA is also required to surrender to the state the areas under its control.

1995 A 7,000-member peacekeeping force, UNAVEM III, is approved for Angola by the UN Security Council.

1997

April	A national reconciliation government is inaugurated under President José Eduardo dos Santos. Jonas Savimbi declines a post in the unity government.
October	The UN imposes sanctions on UNITA for its neglect to abide with the 1994 Lusaka Protocol.

1998 Renewed fighting creates a new refugee crisis. Global Witness, a British based nongovernmental organization, reports that UNITA's war against the government is being financed by massive diamonds sales.

1999 The UN peacekeeping mission ends.

August 9	Independent Roman Catholic radio station Radio Ecclesia is closed by the police.

2002

February 22	UNITA leader Jonas Savimbi is killed by government troops during a commando raid in the eastern province of Moxico.

March	Cease-fire talks begin between UNITA and the government. On April 2, an amnesty bill is passed by parliament that calls for the demobilization of UNITA fighters and their integration into the Angolan armed forces. On April 4, a cease-fire agreement is signed by the government and UNITA.
August 2	The government officially proclaims the end of the war, which has claimed nearly 300,000 people. UNITA officially scraps its armed wing.

2003

January	Fernando da Piedade Dias (Nando) dos Santos is appointed prime minister.
June	Isaias Samakuva becomes president of UNITA, now a political party.

2004

May	The National Assembly passes a law on freedom of conscience, worship, and religion, which guarantees the constitutional right of freedom of religion and unrestricted freedom of churches and other religious bodies to organize and practice their faith within the bounds of the law.

2005

February	The Ministry of Culture inaugurates a commission of 14 specialists to produce a history of Angolan literature.
March–May	Outbreak of the deadly Ebola-like Marburg virus, which kills more than 300 people, particularly in the north. About 75 percent of the victims of the virus are children younger than age five.

2006

June	Angola's national team nicknamed, *Palancas Negras* (Black Antelopes), makes its début in the Soccer World Cup. The team bows out of the finals played in Germany in the first round but returns home to a hero's welcome.

1

Introduction

THE REPUBLIC OF ANGOLA, as it is officially known, is an African nation located in the west-central part of the continent between latitudes 5 degrees and 18 degrees south of the equator and between longitudes 12 degrees and 24 degrees east. It is bounded by the Democratic Republic of the Congo (DRC) in the north and northeast, Zambia in the east, Namibia in the south, and the Atlantic in the west. Angola is one of the large states in the central-southern axis of Africa, about twice the size of the state of Texas, and covers more than 481,354 square miles in land and inland waters. Its territorial limits include Cabinda, about 20 miles from the mainland. Cabinda, with a population of 250,000, is a small but important stretch of land in the north-western tip detached from the mainland and strapped between the DRC and the Republic of the Congo. The capital city of Angola is Luanda, located on the Atlantic coast in the northwestern part of the country. Other important cities include Huambo, Benguela, Lobito, and Lubango.

Angola obtained political independence on November 11, 1975, after nearly fifteen years of armed rebellion against Portuguese colonialism. Colonial rule over the country was not only long it was also severely exploitative and particularly brutal. During the decolonization era in the late 1950s and the early 1960s when colonial powers began to grant independence to African states, Portugal failed to voluntarily relinquish tutelage over its own colonial possessions. The result in Angola, as in Mozambique and Guinea Bissau, was a bloody war of national liberation.

Angola emerged from colonial rule with the expectation of building an economically prosperous state founded on democratic principles of freedom, justice, and the rule of law. Devastated by a brutal civil war that lasted nearly

Map of Africa showing Angola. Cartography by Bookcomp, Inc.

three decades, the nation has been unable to build either a strong economy, or a stable democratic society. The civil war, to a large extent, has indeed defined Angola's modern history. The war began after independence in 1975 when the three major liberation movements that had fought for independence—the Popular Movement for the Liberation of Angola (Movimento Popular de Libertação de Angola, MPLA), the National Front for the Liberation of Angola (Frente Nacional de Libertação de Angola, FNLA), and the National Union for the Total Independence of Angola (União Nacional para a Independência Total de Angola, UNITA)—clashed in a struggle for power. The power struggle between the movements soon turned into a full-scale vicious civil war that was exploited by covert Cold War intervention. Barring a brief period of cease-fire lasting from mid-1991 to late 1992, the war, once described as the "world's deadliest,"[1] ended only in 2002.

The war's adverse effect on every facet of Angola's postindependence life is clearly evident. The human cost of the war can be counted in the enormous wartime loss of life and large-scale population displacement and in the continued postwar deaths and serious injuries inflicted by land mines buried during the war. The war also severely stunted economic growth and the development of necessary social services for the welfare of the people. Medical services, where they are in existence, remain very poor, and the educational system has almost collapsed.

Since the end of the war, however, Angola has launched itself on a path of painfully slow but sure progress. Many people who had fled their homes during the war began to return after the cessation of hostilities to continue their livelihoods. The task of rebuilding has been greatly assisted by humanitarian aid.

Angola is made up of numerous ethnolinguistic groups numbering about a hundred. A few of them are large, whereas others are of medium or small size. The most prominent of the groups are the Ovimbundu, the Mbundu, the Bakongo, the Nganguela (Ganguela), and the Lunda-Chokwe. Smaller groups include the Ovambo, the Nyaneka-Humbe, the Herero, and the Xindonga. There are also a number of small bands of people who were traditionally nomadic or seminomadic hunters and gatherers of wild plants.

Angola's predominant religion is Christianity. The majority of the Christians belong to the Roman Catholic faith, but many others are Protestants. Relations between Catholics and Protestants have not always been very cordial in Angolan history. Christianity is more urban-based, popular among the educated elite and middle classes. Indigenous religious practices are still practiced in many areas, particularly in the rural areas. Islam is restricted to an insignificant minority.

An accurate population figure for Angola is difficult to come by. Nevertheless, according to a 2006 estimate, the population of the country is about 12.1 million, with an annual growth rate of 2.45 percent. With a population density of 27 people per square mile, Angola is rather underpopulated relative to its size. The major reasons for this are the protracted civil war; the high infant mortality rate, which in 2006 was 185.36 deaths per 1,000 live births, representing one of the highest in the world; and the abysmally low life expectancy, which in 2006 was 37.47 years for men and 39.83 for women.[2]

The population of Angola is particularly rural-based. Only about 32 percent of the people are urban dwellers. The population is also unevenly distributed. The north and the coastal stretch boast of about 70 percent of the population. The population is quite youthful, with 45 percent younger than the age of 15 and only 5 percent older than 60 years.

A characteristic of Angola's postindependence demography is large-scale population movement due to the civil war. According to a June 2000 United Nations estimate, about 2.5 million people were displaced internally, and another 2.75milion were in need of humanitarian aid, not counting those in

Major ethnic groups of Angola. Cartography by Bookcomp, Inc.

areas held by UNITA rebels. Also, a significant Angolan refugee population resides in neighboring countries, particularly in Zambia.

LAND

Angola is a vast country, the seventh largest in Africa. Excluding the Cabinda enclave, the country stretches along a thousand miles of the South Atlantic, extending more than another one thousand miles inland to the border of Zambia. Generally, three major features characterize Angola's physical geography: the coastal lowlands, the hills and the mountains, and the great plateau.

In the west along the coast is the lowland plain with low terraces. The lowland varies in width from about thirty miles at its narrowest point in the Benguela area, to more than ninety miles in the north in the Luanda area in the Cuanza (Kwanza) River valley. The plains also extend to some considerable width in the south in the area south of the town of Namibe.

From the coastal lowland, the topography turns into a belt of hills and mountains that extends to about ninety miles in the north and narrows to about twenty miles in the center and in the south. In the northern part of this belt above the Cuanza River, the lowlands gradually turn into hills with elevations averaging 1,500 feet. South of the Cuanza River, the lowlands change more abruptly into hills that form a great escarpment extending downward to the south and through Namibia. The escarpment's highest point is 7,874 feet and is steepest in the Serra da Chela mountain range in Huíla Province.

The third main area of Angola's physical feature is the high plateau *(planalto)*. This is a vast plateau that extends east of the hills and envelopes virtually the rest of the country. The Angolan high plateau is a part of the Central African Plateau system that extends from the southern DRC to Namibia. The plateau elevation averages about 6,000 feet, with higher ranges reaching more than 8,200 feet, as in parts of the Benguela and the Huíla Plateaus. Morro de Moco (8,592 feet), in Huambo Province, is the highest point in Angola.

The vegetation of Angola varies greatly, ranging from grassland to forest and desert. The northern coastline down to the central part of the country is woodland and grassland with patches of evergreen forest. East of this belt, from the north to central Angola, roughly bordered by the central bend of the Cuanza River, is the savannah zone. The rest of the country, particularly the eastern half, is tropical forest and grassland, save for a southwestern desert, the Namib, in the corner along the coastline from Lobito.

Angola has a network of rivers, many of which originate in the central mountains. The major rivers are the Cuanza, Cunene, Cubango, Cuando (Kwando), Cassai (Kasai), Cuito, and Chicapa. The Cuanza and the Cunene flow northward and southward, respectively, but both drain their waters into the Atlantic. The Cuango and the Chicapa both flow northward into the Congo River system in the DRC. The Cuando, Cubango, and Cuito, on the other hand, flow southeastward into the Okavango Swamp in Botswana. With the exception of the Cuanza, which is navigable for about 125 miles from its mouth, Angola's rivers do not serve transportation purposes. The rivers have other utilities, however. For example, the Cuanza and Cunene, which flow westward into the Atlantic, provide water for irrigation in the arid coastal lands. These rivers also have dams that are sources of potential hydroelectric power.

Angola's climate is generally tropical, although local weather may be affected by altitude. The country has two alternating seasons: dry and wet. During the wet season, rainfall is prevalent, and the dry season is drier and characterized by morning mist that may be heavy in many places. The wet season in the north lasts from September to April, and the dry season lasts the remaining months. In the south, the wet season is from November to February, and the dry season lasts the remainder of the year.

The Atlantic's Benguela Current flows along the Angolan coastline and reduces rain and makes the coastal strip arid or semiarid in the south and dry in the north. Precipitation increases toward the east and is highest in the interior uplands.

PEOPLES

Like most African countries, Angola is a multiethnic state. It has a few large and medium-size ethnolinguistic groups and numerous small ones. Except for a few small groups believed to be original to south-central and southern Africa, Angola's ethnic groups are predominantly of Bantu heritage. They were a part of the Bantu migration that began during the first millennium A.D. from the region around southeastern Nigeria and Cameroon to central and southern Africa

The Ovimbundu, the largest ethnolinguistic group in Angola, constitute about 38 percent of the entire population of the country. Speaking a language known as Umbundu, the Ovimbundu live predominantly in the west-central region of Angola, around the Benguela Plateau, where they had migrated from northern and eastern Angola between the sixteenth and the eighteenth centuries. On the fertile plateau, the people built numerous kingdoms, including powerful ones like Bailundu, Bié, Ciyaka, and Wambu, which in the eighteenth century were strong enough to control other kingdoms in the area.

The Ovimbundu emerged during the eighteenth century as the most enterprising traders in the Angolan hinterlands. Through their major kingdoms, they played an active role in the trading systems in central Africa from Benguela on the coast to the interior of modern-day Angola. Particularly, they served as raiders and intermediaries in the Portuguese slave trade in the eighteenth and the nineteenth centuries, organizing raiding expeditions to procure slaves for the Europeans on the coast. By the mid-nineteenth century, they had assumed a prominent place in the Atlantic trade in west-central Africa, having displaced the Imbangala, who had hitherto held a monopoly of slave raiding in conjunction with the Portuguese on the coast.

In the late nineteenth century, the Ovimbundu economy underwent the inevitable change orchestrated by the decline of the Atlantic slave trade. In the era of so-called legitimate trade, economic ventures associated with slave trading gave way to cash-crop production, particularly coffee. The Ovimbundu cash-crop economic venture did not last, however, for long for a variety of reasons, including land appropriation by European settlers.

Meanwhile, by the early twentieth century, the Ovimbundu kingdoms had succumbed to the Portuguese and lost their independence. The Portuguese colonial authority appropriated lands for Europeans, and its unfavorable policies toward Africans forced many Ovimbundu to resort to migrant labor across the country, mostly on European plantations and in industrial areas.

Living north of the Ovimbundu in the northwestern provinces are the Mbundu, speakers of the Kimbundu language. The second largest ethno-linguistic group, the Umbundu number roughly 6 million and constitute about 25 percent of the Angolan population. The people were noted for building one of the most powerful precolonial states of west-central Africa, the Ndongo Kingdom. Established in the fifteenth century, Ndongo was to become a principal slave-trading kingdom. The name *Angola* is believed to have been coined by the Portuguese from one of the earliest Ndongo rulers, Ngola.

The third largest ethnolinguistic group is the Bakongo, representing about 15 percent of the country's population. The Bakongo, who speak Kikongo, live in the north and northwestern parts of Angola, particularly in Uíge and Zaire Provinces, and in Cabinda. The Bakongo are also found in neighboring states; they form the majority of the population in the DRC and are also numerous in the Republic of the Congo.

Much smaller ethnic groups are predominant in Angola. The Lunda and the Chokwe and other related people, noted for their artistic prowess, constitute about 10 percent of Angola's population and are concentrated principally in the area between the Cuango and Cassai Rivers in the Lunda provinces. East and south of the Ovimbundu, and split by the Lunda-Chokwe southward expansion, are the Nganguela (Ganguela), who constitute about 6 percent of the population. The Nyaneka-Humbe (Haneca-Humbe) are located south of the Ovimbundu, and they constitute 3 percent of the population. The Ovambo, making up about 2 percent of the population, live predominantly in Cunene Province in the south-central part of the country bordering Namibia. In the far southwestern corner of Angola in the provinces of Namibe, Benguela, and Huíla are the Herero, representing about 0.5 percent of the population; like the Ovambo, they are also found in larger concentration in Namibia. In the southeastern corner of the country are the Xindonga.

Found in small numbers and scattered in communities in the southern part of Angola, chiefly in the provinces of Kuando-Kubango, Cunene, Namibe, and Huíla, are bands of nomadic hunters, gatherers, and occasional herders believed to be native to the region. Prior to the twentieth century, these groups lived a nomadic or seminomadic life. In this category are Khoisan speakers, who, unlike the so-called Bantu groups, speak a variety of what has been termed *click languages,* derived from their distinctive tonal click sounds. The Khoisan groups are also remarkably different in physical feature from the neighboring groups. They are diminutive in stature and light in complexion. Other hunter-gatherer groups are somewhat different from the Khoisan in that they are more sedentary, characteristically taller, and speak so-called Bantu languages.

Apart from these groups, two important minority groups form part of the Angolan population. One group, representing 1 percent of the total population of the country, is made up of Europeans, particularly Portuguese. The European element in Angola, found mainly in the large coastal cities such as Luanda and Benguela, makes the country a multiracial state.

The second important minority group is the *mestiço*, people of mixed European and African origins. Interracial mixing was a feature of precolonial Angola resulting, in the early twentieth century, in a *mestiço* population that exceeded that of Europeans. Although there are rural *mestiços*, most live in urban areas and are educated. During the colonial period, many *mestiços* were able to attain the status of assimilated persons *(assimilados)*. This was a status conferred on non-Europeans who had fulfilled a number of requirements under the Portuguese policy of assimilation and were thus eligible for Portuguese citizenship. As Angolans assimilated into the Portuguese culture, the *mestiços* generally identified with Portuguese ways of life and sought a status truly on a par with Europeans. The vast majority of Angolans, the *indigenas*, who remained unassimilated, had deep resentment for the *mestiços*. The *mestiços* now constitute about 2 percent of the population of Angola.

There is a difference in the level of Westernization and urbanization among Angola's ethnic groups. Those who live near the coast had greater interaction with the Portuguese, and thus more exposure to their influence than interior groups in the south and the east. For instance, the Western Mbundu, around their chief city Luanda and other cities such as Malanje, are the most urbanized and Westernized people in Angola, having been long exposed to strong Portuguese influences. During the colonial period, many of the urbanized Mbundu adopted Portuguese lifestyles, acquired Western education and religion, and thus became qualified as *assimilados*. Many intermarried with the Portuguese, producing *mestiços*.

LANGUAGES

Portuguese is the lingua franca of Angola, a language bequeathed by the erstwhile colonial power, Portugal. Besides the official language, various African languages are spoken throughout the country, each of them containing a number of dialects. Most Angolans speak their mother tongue, first and foremost. The most widely spoken languages are Umbundu, Kimbundu, and Kikongo.

EDUCATION

Western education is greatly valued in Angola, and it is seen as a means to enhance social and economic status. Thus, high priority is placed on the education of children by their parents. At independence in 1975, educational reforms were introduced to reverse the colonial educational system that neglected black education. The reforms provided for instructions in Angolan indigenous languages; more importantly, however, they focused on promoting literacy. Free and compulsory primary and secondary education became state policy to help enhance the literacy level and reduce adult illiteracy, which at independence was greater than 85 percent. The educational reforms brought about increased student enrollment, particularly at the primary and secondary school levels but also at the university level.

Although educational reforms have reduced the illiteracy level in Angola, the country's educational system has not produced significant results. The financially strapped Angolan government has been unable to adequately cater to the educational needs of the populace. Throughout much of its history as an independent state, Angola has expended enormous resources on defense rather than on social services, including education. The government funding of education has thus been grossly inadequate. Lack of necessary educational equipment and infrastructure throughout Angola has greatly devalued the quality of education in the country. Primary education, with inadequate classrooms and other facilities as well as trained teachers, is of very poor quality. In 2000, only about 45 percent of school-age children attended school. The teacher-pupil ratio is extremely high, sometimes one teacher to eighty pupils, and the rate of school dropout is very high.

For many Angolans, higher education is out of reach as only a few people can afford the cost. In 2005, the Angolan Ministry of Education named seven government-recognized institutions of higher learning in the country, two of them public and five private. The major public institution is the Agostinho Neto University (Universidade de Agostinho Neto, UAN) in Luanda, with branches in Huambo and Lubango. The university was established in 1962 as part of Estudos Gerais Universitários de Angola, a Portuguese system of higher education. In 1968, it became the autonomous University of Luanda (Universidade de Luanda) and was subsequently renamed the University of Angola (Universidade de Angola) in 1976; in 1985, it acquired its present name of Universidade de Agostinho Neto, in honor of the late President Neto. The university has departments of agriculture, education, economics, engineering, law, medicine, and sciences, among others. The other public institution is the Institute of International Relations in Luanda.

School children. Many children in Angola do not have access to education. Primary school enrollment has progressively dropped over the years. Many of the children who start primary school do not complete their education. Courtesy of Armando J. Rodriguez, Jr.

Of the private higher institutions, the most prominent is the Catholic University (Universidade Católica de Angola, UCAN), also in Luanda, which opened effectively in 1999 and teaches subjects such as business, sciences, computer sciences, economics, and law. Other private institutions include Universidade Jean Piaget de Angola, Universidade Lusíada de Angola, Universidade Independente de Angola, and Instituto Superior Privado de Angola, all of which offer a variety of science, engineering, humanities, and professional courses.

Angola's institutions of higher education are often poorly equipped in terms of modern facilities. Even the Huambo campus of the Agostinho Neto University was closed down a number of times during the civil war. The post-secondary institutions in Angola are also few and are not in much better shape in terms of facilities. A major effect of the lack of a good educational system in Angola is that the country still has a very low literacy rate: 42 percent.

CITIES

Luanda, the capital of Angola and its administrative seat, has a long history dating back to the late sixteenth century. It was founded by the Portuguese in 1575 and subsequently became the center of the Atlantic slave trade in central Africa. From Luanda, hundreds of enslaved Africans were shipped out of central Africa to the New World, particularly Brazil. Today, Luanda is Angola's largest city and its chief port and major business center. Its major industry is oil refinery, but a few light industries also exist, such as cement manufacturing, textiles, plastics, and cigarettes.

Luanda is also a historic city and is Angola's main social and cultural center. Portuguese influence is evident as many of the buildings are a legacy of Portugal's colonial rule. The city is popular for its many cultural attractions such as museums and for its social activities, including a popular carnival featuring the sensuous dance, semba.

When Angola obtained independence in 1975, the population of Luanda was no more than 700,000. Rural-urban migration over the years has, however, turned the city into a sprawling urban center. During the civil war, Luanda experienced a steady influx of refugees fleeing war-affected rural areas. Luanda currently has an estimated population of about 4 million. The population explosion has led to overcrowding with a resultant severe problem of inadequate social services such as sanitation, treated water, and uninterrupted electricity. Dotted around the city are shantytowns *(musseques)*, the abode of the displaced and other poor people where squalor and diseases are the order of the day.

Inland, on a plateau in agriculturally rich west-central Angola, and about 300 miles east of Luanda is Huambo, the nation's second largest city and the administrative capital of Huambo Province. Formally called Nova Lisboa (New Lisbon), Huambo is a bustling urban center with a population of about 250,000 people. It is a major road, rail, and air transport center in southern Africa. Its roads and rail lines link major coastal cities such as Luanda and Lobito and also serve the eastern interior and the DRC, Zambia, and Namibia. The city is a commercial center as well, and shipping is an important industry. Huambo's export products include fruit, grain, hides, rice, and skins.

Huambo particularly bore the brunt of destruction and brutality during the civil war. The city was besieged by UNITA rebel forces in 1993 and again in 1998. The attacks left in their wake a litany of deaths and displacement of populations.

Lobito, an urban center of about 150,000 people was founded by the Portuguese in 1843. It is located in west-central Angola on the Atlantic Ocean. It is Angola's most important port after Luanda, and it also serves as the western terminus of the trans-African Benguela railroad. This vitally important railroad, which was completed in 1929, has transformed the city into a leading commercial center by connecting it with the mines in the DRC and Zambia.

High-rise buildings and broad, palm tree-lined boulevards are a feature of some Angolan major cities such as Luanda. Courtesy of Armando J. Rodriguez, Jr.

Also on the Atlantic in western Angola is Benguela, a city of 155,000 people and the administrative capital of Benguela Province. The city was founded in 1617 and was the principal slave-trading port of the Atlantic slave trade apart from Luanda. From this port, the Ovimbundu controlled the southern sector of the slave trade in west-central Africa. Today, Benguela is a principal commercial center in Angola, a terminus of the Benguela railroad, and a major outlet for export commodities.

Angola's other important cities include the ports of Namibe and Cabinda and the inland city of Lubango. Namibe (formerly called Mossamedes) is located in the south along the coast and noted for the production of cotton, tobacco, sisal, frozen meat, hides, and skins and the export of iron ore. Cabinda, the chief city in the Cabinda enclave, is noted for its enormous oil resources and oil exploration. Lubango (formerly Sá Da Bandeira), located in the southwestern part of Angola, is a railroad city and the administrative capital of Huíla Province.

Angolan cities, like the country as a whole, were hard hit by the protracted civil war. The war caused untold infrastructural damage in many cities. Luanda, for instance, a beautiful city once referred to as the "Paris of Africa," lost much of its glory after the war. The ports of Benguela and Lobito were adversely affected by the massive damage done to the Benguela Railroad during the war, which rendered a great portion of it unusable. The war expenses, which gulped the lion's share of the country's resources, did not allow timely repairs to damaged facilities; neither did they allow room for capital development projects. Angola's substandard roads went from bad to worse because of neglect; utilities and communication systems degenerated and became inadequate or even nonexistent in some places. Nevertheless, Angolan cities today are making strides in reconstruction. Infrastructures are slowly being rehabilitated; road and rail lines are being repaired.

RESOURCES, OCCUPATIONS, AND ECONOMY

Angola is vastly endowed with resources, both mineral and agricultural. Mining is an important economic enterprise and one of the nation's chief sources of income. Rich oil deposits are found in the northwestern part of the country, and the major oil terminals are located in Luanda, Malongo (Cabinda), Palanca, and Quinfuquena. Angola is the second largest producer of crude oil in Africa (after Nigeria). According to government sources, new discoveries have been made, and the country is said to have oil reserves up to 5.4 billion barrels.

Oil exploration began in Angola in the 1960s, largely handled by foreign companies such as BP Amoco, ChevronTexaco, ExxonMobil, Shell, AGIP, and Total. Exploration has rapidly expanded, and today the oil and gas industry is the most important sector of the economy, constituting about 90 percent of total exports and contributing about 45 percent of the gross domestic product (GDP). A state-owned corporation, the Sociedade Nacional de Combustiveis de Angola (Sonangol), created in 1976, oversees the management of the oil sector.

Second to oil in importance are diamonds, which were discovered in 1912. The central province of Bié and the northeast provinces of Lunda Norte and Lunda Sul are rich in the mineral. Prior to independence, Angola was the world's fourth largest producer of diamonds after Botswana, Russia, and South Africa. Angola's diamond company is Sociedade de Comercialização de Diamantes (Sodiam), but production is principally handled by foreign companies such as DiamondWorks and Ashton Mining Company. During the civil war, illicit diamond trafficking was the order of the day. The UNITA rebels particularly exploited captured mines that enabled them to continue their prosecution of the war. Since the end of the war, more stringent state control of the diamond industry has been introduced with the aim of regularizing production and increasing exploitation. Although the illegal diamond trade has been reduced, it has not been eliminated.

Other mineral resources constitute a vital part of the Angolan economy. Iron ore is also a leading product, but commercial production fell during the civil war as a result of destruction of mines. Angola also produces copper, gold, phosphates, manganese, bauxite, lead, zinc, and uranium.

Adequate arable land in Angola ensures a variety of agricultural resources, both for export and subsistence purposes. Coffee is the most important export crop produced in the northern part of Angola. Other export crops include sisal, timber, cotton, palm produce, bananas, sugarcane, corn, and tobacco. Subsistence agriculture, which accounts for less than 15 percent of Angola's GDP, is nevertheless important. The vast majority of Angolans—close to 90 percent of the population—are engaged in this sec-

Street hawking of a variety of wares is an important aspect of the informal market. Here a hawker sells bananas amidst traffic. Courtesy of Armando J. Rodriguez, Jr.

tor of the economy, which provides them their main source of livelihood. The main subsistence agricultural products are cassava (manioc), plantains, and vegetables.

In addition to forest products, livestock and fishing are an integral part of the Angolan economy. Animal husbandry, especially cattle, sheep, goats, and pigs, is popular in the savannah regions of the country. The coastline of Angola, rich in maritime life as a result of the cool offshore Benguela current, makes the region important for fishing activities. Indeed, Angola is a noted exporter of fish products and a variety of fish such as mackerel, tuna, shellfish, and sardines. Foreign corporations are active in the buoyant Angolan fishing industry.

Foreign trade is an important component of Angola's economy. The nation exports major raw materials such as crude oil and refined petroleum products, gas, diamonds, coffee, timber, cotton, and fish and fish products. Angola's total exports in 2003 were $9.7 billion and were mainly to Western and Asian countries.[3] The United States has recently emerged as Angola's leading trade partner and has displaced Portugal as the primary export destination. The steady rise in U.S. trade with Angola is evident in that almost one-fifth of all its imports from Africa are from Angola. In 2003, the U.S. imports from Angola reached about $4.3 billion.[4] Its major import is oil, a sector in which U.S. oil companies have been very active. Besides oil, however, the United States also imports chemicals and related products and other minerals and metals from Angola. Angola's other major exports partners include Germany, the United Kingdom, France, the Netherlands, Belgium, Spain, China, Taiwan, and Japan.

Lacking an industrial manufacturing base, Angola's external trade also involves large-scale imports of manufactured goods. Its leading import partner is still Portugal, followed by the United States, Brazil, France, Spain, and the Netherlands. Imports range from automobiles and other heavy machinery, including spare parts and military hardware, to electronics, medicines, textiles, and foodstuffs. In 2003, Angola's imports amounted to more than $4 billion.[5]

The wealth of resources in Angola has not translated into economic development and prosperity, however, and the economy remains rather undeveloped. During the civil war, the Angolan currency, the kwanza, which replaced the escudo in 1977, was repeatedly devalued, causing living standard to further tumble. Although mismanagement of public funds and resources partly accounted for economic underdevelopment, the primary factor was the devastating civil war, which gulped the wealth from the nation's vast resources. The government expended huge oil revenues to prosecute the war, and revenues from illegal diamond mining and exports largely supported the rebel UNITA forces. Thus, for about a quarter of a century, the lion's share of Angola's resources went into military expenditure. For most of the 1990s, Angola topped Africa in arms imports, spending $1.2 billion on the purchase of military hardware and weapons in 1997.[6]

Angola has a mixed economic system in which the public and private sectors coexist in spite of the many years of rule by the left-leaning MPLA government. The private sector chiefly comprises small-scale enterprises; most of the large-scale industries are government-controlled. Industrial development is less than modest; by 2000, the production growth rate was at an abysmally low 1 percent. The major manufacturing industries are natural gas production, metalwork, textiles, cement and glass production, beverage brewing, and fish and food processing. Foreign interests have largely been active in the exploitation of the nation's mineral resources, particularly in the oil sector.

Economic underdevelopment in Angola after almost thirty years of independence is evident in its lack of adequate basic infrastructure, such as a good transportation system, housing, and education, and adequate healthcare delivery. Because industrial production is greatly retarded, Angola relies heavily on importation of virtually every needed commodity. Most people, about 85 percent of the population, are engaged in petty trading and subsistence farming. With a large number of amputees, victims of land mines, and refugees displaced from their homes, a significant proportion of the Angolan population is unemployed. As a result of this high unemployment rate, poverty is rampant; indeed, more than 80 percent of the people live in poverty.

Food scarcity is a particularly urgent problem in Angola. During the war years, farming was disrupted in virtually all of Angola, which led to famine in many parts of the country. Since the war ended, however, the major agricultural preoccupation of Angolans—subsistence farming—still faces production problems. Infrastructure is lacking, and most often seeds must be imported, which has driven up food prices. Indeed, food crises have been reported in many parts of the country, most especially among rural populations inaccessible to local government officials due to bad road conditions. In late 2003 in Camacua district, for example, the people of Umpulo facing food scarcity were said to have resorted to eating wild animals, honey, and mushrooms.[7] The work of a number of international aid agencies, however, has to some extent ameliorated some of Angola's acute economic and social problems. These agencies have helped provide food and medical supplies in places where they are needed most.

Nevertheless, the Angolan economy has made some strides since the cessation of hostilities in 2002. The government has embarked on an economic reform program to stabilize the economy and thus alleviate poverty. State control of the economy has eased, and many state-owned enterprises have been privatized. Private investment is also encouraged, and a public accounting system is emphasized to curtail rampant corruption. The government has succeeded in reducing inflation from 325 percent in 2000 to about 106 percent in 2002, and further reduction has been seen. Angola has also been able to bring down external debt from an all-time high of $10.5 billion in 1999 to $9.2 billion in 2003.[8] External trade has increased significantly; presently, the third largest market for the United States in Africa is Angola, after South Africa and Nigeria. With Angola's wealth of natural resources, the potential for rapid economic development is great if the resources are properly managed.

GOVERNMENT

After independence in 1975, Angola became a one-party state. Ostensibly, the independence constitution of November 11, 1975 (which has been revised a number of times)[9] established a democratic state based on the rule of law and, therefore, a guarantee of basic civil and political rights to the citizens. The constitution entrusts power to the people through a representative form of government, and an electoral process provides for periodic elections and universal adult suffrage.

The government of Angola is headed by a president who is the chief executive of state, commander in chief of the armed forces, and the head of government. Elected by an absolute majority vote in a direct election, the president's term of office is five years, with eligibility for reelection for another term. The president presides over an executive branch of the government comprising the prime minister, cabinet ministers, secretaries of state, and other state officials. The prime minister occupies a nominal position and is responsible to the president, to whom he reports regularly and directly on matters of national policy. The major departments are those of Education and Culture, National Defense, and National Police and are headed by the president's appointees.

A 220-member unicameral legislative body, the National Assembly, enacts state laws. One hundred thirty members of the assembly are elected by proportional vote and the rest from provincial districts for four-year terms. The judicial system is largely based on the Portuguese legal system with the infusion of elements of customary law. The Supreme Court is the highest

Administrative units of Angola. Cartography by Bookcomp, Inc.

court with jurisdiction over the entire nation. The legal system recently has been modified to accommodate political pluralism and the demands of a free-enterprise economy.

Administrative Divisions

Administratively, Angola is divided into provinces, each of which is further subdivided into councils and communes. The 18 provinces are headed by governors appointed by the president. The ruling MPLA is represented by a state official at every level of local government. For many years after independence, the government was unable to exercise authority over the whole of the country, and thus some provinces were unofficially held by UNITA. Following is a list of the 18 Angolan provinces and their capital cities.

Province	Capital
Bengo	Caxito
Benguela	Benguela
Bié	Kuito
Cabinda	Cabinda
Cuando Cubango	Menongue
Cuanza Norte	N'Dalatando
Cuanza Sul	Sumbe
Cunene	Ondjiva
Huambo	Huambo
Huíla	Lubango
Luanda	Luanda
Lunda Norte	Lucapa
Lunda Sul	Saurimo
Malanje	Malanje
Moxico	Luena
Namibe	Namibe
Uíge	Uíge
Zaire	M'Banza Kongo

Political Parties and Party Politics

As a one-party state until 1992, Angola's political system was, in reality, less than democratic. Since independence in 1975, the ruling party has been the MPLA, first under the nation's first president, Agostinho Neto, and since September 1979 under its current president, José Eduardo dos Santos. President dos Santos, who has been in power for more than twenty-five years, initially assumed power without opposition. Angola's first ever multiparty election occurred only in September 1992, which, in a disputed result, retained the ruling MPLA. Opposition elements have recently begun to call for fresh polls to elect a new National Assembly and a new president. Although a constitutional committee had been set up by dos Santo to address the modus operandi of new elections, as of mid-2004 the government had not yet issued an election schedule nor had it created an electoral commission.

The MPLA is justifiably the most prominent political party in Angola given its sole control of power for the last quarter of a century. The party originated as a guerrilla movement founded in 1956 to fight for Angola's independence. When Angola became independent in 1975, the MPLA was transformed into a political party and its leader, Agostinho Neto, became the president of the republic. The MPLA formally adopted a Marxist-Leninist ideology in 1977 and rechristened itself the Popular Movement for the Liberation of Angola–Labor Party (Partido do Trabalho, MPLA-PT). From 1975, Angola's politics was dominated by the MPLA. Election contests were primarily only between candidates who were card-carrying members of the party. In April 1991, the MPLA formally renounced Marxism as official state policy and opened the way for free-market enterprise.

UNITA, the second largest party in Angola and formed in 1966, was initially a guerrilla movement, one of the three principal movements that fought Portuguese colonialism. Its founder was Jonas Savimbi, one of the most controversial political leaders in Angola. UNITA lost out to the MPLA in the postindependence power struggle, and although it had fought the liberation war with the MPLA, it quickly became a rebel organization that would engage the MPLA government in armed resistance from 1975 almost nonstop until 2002.

In a cease-fire agreement between the MPLA and UNITA in 1991, the government recognized UNITA as a legitimate political party and allowed it to participate in the multiparty elections for president and parliament the following year. In the elections held on September 29 and 30, the MPLA won 54 percent of the votes and UNITA 43 percent. In the presidential election, dos Santos won 49.6 percent of the votes, defeating Savimbi who won 40.1 percent.[10] The MPLA victory did not go well with UNITA. Claiming widespread electoral fraud, Savimbi disputed and rejected the election results and withdrew UNITA from scheduled runoff election. The cease-fire collapsed thereafter, and Angola slipped back into hostilities.

Nevertheless, a modicum of democracy continued to exist in the form of multipartyism in the National Assembly, where a number of smaller political parties were able to win seats. Indeed, Angola boasts of an array of small parties with the political spectrum raging from conservative to authoritarian and extreme left. In addition to the better known FNLA, originally a nationalist movement founded in 1962 by Holden Roberto to fight the war of liberation against Portugal, other smaller parties include the Aliança Democrática de Angola (Democratic Alliance of Angola), Fórum Democrático Angolano (Angolan Democratic Forum), Partido Democrático para Progreso/Aliança Nacional Angolano (Democratic Progress Party/Angolan National Alliance party), Partido Liberal Democrático (Liberal Democratic Party), Partido Nacional Democrático Angolano (Angolan National Democratic Party), Partido Renovador Social (Social Renewal Party), Partido Renovador Democrático (Democratic Renewal Party), Partido Social-Democrata (Social Democrat Party), Partido Republicano de Angola (Republican Party of

Angola), and União Democrática Nacional de Angola (National Democratic Union of Angola).

Under Angola's one-party system, violation of human rights was rife. Political opposition was not tolerated and opposition elements and dissenters were regularly persecuted. The war years, especially the latter period, saw massive human rights abuses perpetrated by both sides of the conflict. Indiscriminate killings, arbitrary arrests and jailing, impressments (particularly of children), rape, and other forms of abuses were rampant.

HISTORY

Early History

Little is known about present-day Angola in the Stone Age period. What is generally known is that the territory was originally inhabited by a number of hunter-gatherer Khoisan groups. The material culture of these autochthonous groups was rather very simple. They did not build centralized states or complex political systems. Their economic preoccupation centered mainly on hunting wild animals in the forests and gathering wild fruits. Some evolved animal husbandry, however, rearing sheep and cattle.[11]

Between the seventh and the thirteenth centuries, new groups, the so-called Bantu, arrived in the Angolan region and displaced the original inhabitants. The newcomers ruled the area until the arrival of the first Europeans, the Portuguese, in the late fifteenth century.

Kingdoms and States

The precolonial people of Angola built states and kingdoms, some large and powerful and others small. The states generally possessed a centralized political authority in which a ruler exercised power and legislated for the people, assisted by chiefs. Most states possessed an army with which the ruler fought battles to expand or defend his kingdom. Indeed, precolonial Angola experienced a lot of interstate conflicts, particularly stemming from trade rivalry. The competition over the control of the slave trade with the Europeans on the coast was a constant factor for friction.

Ndongo was the most powerful and most enterprising state of precolonial Angola. For some time, it rivaled the Kongo Kingdom, the most impressive state of southwestern Africa located farther north in the present-day DRC. The Ndongo Kingdom, founded in the fifteenth century, was famous for its string of powerful women rulers. The first of these women rulers and the most famous was Nzinga Mbande, a warrior who reigned from about 1582 to 1663. Nzinga seized the throne during a succession dispute in 1624 and, according to some accounts, ruled as a bloodthirsty tyrant who indulged in indiscriminate killing of her subjects. To others, however, she was a heroine who establishment a formidable, well-trained army with which she fought many wars, especially against Portuguese expansionism in the Angolan region. Nzinga's reign was an example of early African resistance to European imperial design in Africa.

By the early sixteenth century, a number of Mbundu kingdoms had emerged, notably Matamba and Kasanje, both located east of Ndongo. Though Matamba, on the Kwango River, was independent, it occasionally offered tribute to the powerful Kongo Kingdom. For most of its history up until the nineteenth century, Matamba was engaged in conflict with the Portuguese to reduce their influence in the kingdom. Although Kasanje was a Mbundu kingdom, for the most part it was ruled by the Imbangala. Other notable precolonial states were those established by the Ovimbundu, which included Bié, Bailundu, and Ciyaka.

The Era of the Slave Trade

The Portuguese were the first Europeans to maintain an active presence in Africa. In the fifteenth century, they arrived on the continent as explorers and subsequently explored the west coast of Africa from the Cape Verde Island to Angola. Subsequently, they established themselves on the coast of the Kongo Kingdom and maintained trading and diplomatic relations with the state. Initially, their trading interest was in precious metals such as copper.

Mission work was another initial Portuguese preoccupation, especially among the Kongolese. Missionaries kept close relations to the court of the Manikongo, the ruler of the Kongo Kingdom. Such relations were to culminate in the conversion to Christianity of the Manikongo, Nzinga Nkuwu, and his successor, Nzinga Mbemba, who was christened Afonso I. Proselytizing in the Kongo appeared to have reached beyond the king's court to the commoners. Conversion to Roman Catholicism among the Kongolese was widespread even in the fifteenth century.[12]

By the early sixteenth century, the Portuguese had practically abandoned the quest for precious metals, and their primary interest was now in the trade of slaves with interior groups of central Africa. Farther south, the Portuguese found in Angola a fertile ground for the procurement of slaves for their New World colony. Luanda, which they founded in 1575, was their principal slave-trading port, although it fell to the Dutch briefly in the middle of the seventeenth century. An estimated 4 million people were exported from Angola between 1500 and 1850.[13]

The Colonial Era

Even though the Portuguese had established themselves on the Angolan coast around Luanda by the late fifteenth century, it was not until the early twentieth century that Portugal began to exert formal colonial authority over the area that today constitutes Angola. This followed the conquest of many groups like the Mbundu, the Ovimbundu, the Chokwe, and the Bié, which had militarily resisted Portuguese incursion for centuries until the twentieth century. For instance, the Mbundu resistance finally collapsed in 1902, the Ovimbundu's in 1903, and the Chokwe's in 1914.[14]

Following the subjugation of the people of Angola, Portugal established a formal administrative apparatus to exercise colonial control. It set up political, economic, and social institutions similar to the ones in Portugal. Lisbon's colonial ideology was assimilation, a policy by which Portugal sought to transform Angola along Portuguese lines of development. The policy aimed at assimilating the people of Angola into the supposedly superior Portuguese culture. Also, Angola would be made a province of Portugal and its people granted Portuguese citizenship.

In 1951, Angola was officially declared an overseas province of Portugal. In theory, Angolans were now so-called black Portuguese who could claim the same civil and political rights as other Portuguese citizens living in Portugal. This meant they could elect their own representatives into the Portuguese parliament in Lisbon. In practice, however, very few Angolans were ever assimilated into the Portuguese culture and granted Portuguese citizenship. For the main part in colonial Angola, these *assimilados* did not possess real political power, but they enjoyed far more privileges than the vast majority of Angolans who remained unassimilated. The *indigenas,* as the unassimilated Angolans were called, were without basic civil and political rights and were subjected to a variety of racist laws and forced labor.

Portugal's colonial system in Africa was backward, brutal, and inherently racist. Although the colonial power virulently exploited Angola's human and material resources, it denied Angolans much of the benefits of the wealth of their country. For instance, the system severely limited educational opportunities so that at independence in 1975, literacy level was very low. Also, the colonial system did not provide adequate social services to benefit the colonized people.[15]

Unlike other European colonial empires, the British and the French colonies, for instance, where nationalist activities began after World War II, nationalism was late in commencing in the Portuguese colonies. What was partly responsible for this was the Portuguese repressive colonial system that outlawed any opposition to colonial authority and brutally repressed anticolonial agitation.

Initially, Portugal did not encourage the immigration of white settlers to Angola. This situation changed, however, after Angola was officially declared Portugal's overseas province in 1951. Portuguese settlers began to arrive thereafter in large numbers, and although Angolans were subjected to subordinate position and treated as second-class citizens, the settlers were granted special political and economic privileges. Particularly important was the settlers' control of land through a system of land appropriation by the colonial government. Large-scale land appropriation turned the most fertile lands over to the settlers, and the primary role of Angolans in the colonial economy was to provide labor on European farms. On the eve of Angolan independence, about half a million Portuguese and other Europeans had made Angola their permanent home. Angola was effectively a settler colony like the other Portuguese colonies of Mozambique and Guinea Bissau.

The War of Independence

Portugal's retrogressive colonial system in Angola not only delayed anticolonial agitations, it also made armed struggle inevitable. The colonial authority's intolerance of anticolonial expression only served the purpose of driving nationalist agitation underground. Nationalist organizations began to form from the late 1950s and, because of colonial repression, were based outside Angola and operated in exile. Anticolonial sentiment finally exploded in 1961 when a popular nationalist uprising occurred. Brutally suppressed by the Portuguese army, it reinforced in Angola's nationalist leaders, many of whom had been forced into exile in neighboring states, the inevitability of armed struggle.

The subsequent armed struggle that would eventually lead to Angola's independence in 1975 was championed by three main revolutionary movements: the MPLA, the FLNA, and UNITA. The Marxist-oriented MPLA was established in 1956 by Agostinho Neto and was initially based in neighboring Zambia. In February 1961, it commenced an armed struggle against the Portuguese to end its colonial rule in Angola. The FNLA, another exiled movement organized in the Congo in 1962 by Holden Roberto, joined the struggle. UNITA emerged in 1966 under Jonas Savimbi to become the third main guerrilla organization involved in the war of independence. These nationalist movements employed their military wings to engage the Portuguese in one of the most bloody guerrilla wars in African history.

Portugal responded to the liberation war with an iron fist. For the most part, militarily the war did not go well for the Angolans. Even in the first year of the struggle, Angola's war casualties had numbered almost 50,000, and another half-million people had fled into the DRC, Angola's less impressive military showing could be attributed to two main factors. First, the liberation armies were no match for Portugal's effective counterinsurgency campaigns, which relied on superior military technology and firepower. Second, the guerrilla movements lacked real unity of purpose and strategy in confronting the Portuguese. Rather than coordinating efforts to fight the common enemy,

A young boy sporting on his T-shirt the image of
the celebrated Argentine-born Cuban revolutionary, Che Guevara. The irrepressible Guevara was a
popular icon in Angola during its war of liberation
and was an inspiration to the nationalists. Courtesy
of Armando J. Rodriguez, Jr.

each movement made use of its own armed force. The movements suffered
from a lack of unity as a result of not only ethnic and regional differences but
also political and ideological differences. The three movements did not have
a national outlook and appeal; each derived its support from different ethnic
groups and regions. The MPLA had its power base in the coastal northwest
among the Umbundu. Its Marxist inclination ran counter to the liberal lais-
sez-faire ideology of the FNLA and UNITA. Both the FNLA and UNITA
themselves had their own regional appeal and power base. The FNLA was a
north-central based organization popular among the Kongo. UNITA, on the
other hand, derived its support and strength largely from among the Ovimbundu of the central provinces. Added to the disunity among the nationalist
movements were the rivalry among their leadership and the pursuit of personal agendas. The inability to forge a common front among the nationalist

movements during the war of independence would spill over to the postindependence period and plunge Angola into a civil war.

Portugal's military superiority over the guerrilla forces did not necessarily translate into victory on the battleground for the colonial power. The war did not go well for the nationalists either, but they persisted in the struggle. An event far away from the front would change the dynamics of the war, however. On April 25, 1974, a coup d'état by the Portuguese armed forces overthrew the government of Portugal's Prime Minister Marcelo Caetano. In part, the uprising in Lisbon was orchestrated by the enormous human and material cost to Portugal of the liberation wars going on in the Portuguese empire in Africa. Not only was Angola at war with the colonial power but Mozambique was as well. The apparent inability of the Portuguese army to defeat the guerrillas had begun to make the wars rather unpopular in Portugal. The armed forces bearing the brunt of the fighting were becoming war-weary and suffered mounting casualties. The ordinary taxpayer paying the tab for the conflict was disillusioned by the war that could not be won militarily.

Portugal's new government correctly gauged the temperament of the home front and the reality of the inevitability of Angola's independence. In a move borne out of the realization of the futility of continued suppression of the independence aspiration of Angolans, the government negotiated a truce with the nationalists in May 1974 to conduct peace talks that would bring an end to the drawn-out war. Following the cease-fire, the peace talks led to the Alvir Agreement of January 1975 in which Portugal agreed to Angola's independence. On November 11, 1975, Angola's independence became a reality.

The Angolan Civil War

By the Alvir Agreement that paved the way for Angola's independence in 1975, the three main nationalist movements agreed to a government of national unity in which the movements would share power. This arrangement was not to be because shortly after independence was proclaimed the three liberation movements embarked on the warpath against each other. In the postwar power struggle, the MPLA took control of the government, and its leader, Agostinho Neto, assumed office in Luanda as the first president of independent Angola.

The other two nationalist movements, the FNLA and UNITA, formed a coalition government based in Huambo and opposed the MPLA in a bloody conflict. Although the MLPA government in Luanda was in control of much of the country by 1976, it was unable to immediately defeat the FNLA and UNITA forces. In 1984, however, the FNLA dropped out of the war, but UNITA continued the war with vicious fury and gained sizable areas of the country, particularly in the interior.

The MPLA received the recognition of the Organization of African Unity (OAU) as the legitimate government of Angola. This was a major diplomatic boost for the government as it could now count on critical African support and recognition by most countries of the world. The war was far from being an African affair, however; superpower Cold War politics exploited the conflict. The MPLA with its ideological Marxist leaning received diplomatic and military support from the Soviet Union, Eastern bloc nations, and Communist Cuba in the 1970s and 1980s. The United States, on the other hand, threw its support to the FNLA and UNITA and supplied them military hardware. When the FNLA ceased to be a force in the war, the United States in the late 1980s continued to provide UNITA with military support. Washington, DC, perceived the Marxist-oriented MPLA as an instrument in the hands of the Kremlin to spread Soviet ideology in the strategically important region of southern Africa. It thus sought to use UNITA as a bulwark against Soviet influence. UNITA also received support from troops of apartheid South Africa.

The war gained momentum and began to have immediate repercussions on the nation. The economy was quickly affected by the large-scale flight of Europeans with their technical know-how and investments. The economy

Destruction to physical structure in Angola is a visible legacy of the long civil war. The picture shows a damaged building of the Quéssua theological school, Malange. Courtesy of Armando J. Rodriguez, Jr.

deteriorated rapidly as production slackened and all available resources went to service the war. A massive refugee problem compounded the economic situation as large populations became displaced and many people fled into neighboring states, particularly the DRC.

In March 1991, the warring factions achieved a cease-fire, and the MPLA government agreed to a multiparty Angola. Consequently, all political parties, including UNITA, were legally recognized. In the multiparty elections held in September 1992, Eduardo dos Santos was victorious, and the MPLA carried the majority of seats in parliament. The president's victory and Jonas Savimbi's rejection of the UN-supervised elections because of alleged electoral fraud plunged the nation back into war. The renewed war, much more destructive, dragged on until November 1994 when the two sides drew up another peace proposal. In May 1995, the new peace agreement, the Lusaka Protocol, was signed in Zambia by dos Santos and Savimbi.

By the time of the Lusaka Protocol, UNITA had been severely weakened, a factor that undoubtedly forced Savimbi to the peace table. By the accord, UNITA agreed to a plan for the demobilization and disarmament of its soldiers and the integration of its senior officers into the Angolan armed forces. The accord also stipulated the extension of the authority of the Angolan government over UNITA-controlled areas. The implementation of the accord was to be done under the auspices of a UN peacekeeping force that arrived in Angola in June 1995.

The Lusaka Protocol did not endure, however. Demobilization of troops by UNITA did not go as envisaged nor was the integration of its troops into the Angolan armed forces fully realized. Although in 1997 a new coalition government, the Government of Unity and National Reconciliation (GURN), which included elements of the UNITA cadre, was formed, peace, stability, and security did not return to Angola. In 1998, the cease-fire collapsed and hostilities resumed. The MPLA subsequently suspended the coalition government, blaming UNITA for noncompliance with its Lusaka Protocol obligations. The government also declared Savimbi a persona non grata and thereafter refused to deal with him while working with a new UNITA leadership under a splinter group, UNITA-Renovada.[16]

The renewed war did not go well for UNITA, and by late 1999 government forces were taking the upper hand. UNITA was partly weakened because the revenue it had previously derived from diamond sales that had sustained its war effort was seriously curtailed by a new international embargo on the sale of conflict diamonds. What brought the war to a conclusive end, however, was the death of the UNITA leader, Jonas Savimbi, in battle on February 22, 2002. Following the demise of its leader, UNITA signed a cease-fire agreement with the government. The more than a quarter-century bloody and vicious Angolan civil war thus ended with enormous postwar challenges.

Post–Civil War Period

The human and material costs of the Angolan civil war were unimaginable. The war had claimed some 2 million lives and displaced millions more, giving rise to a massive refugee problem, and fueled mistrust and bad blood between groups. It also had led to nationwide infrastructural damage as roads, bridges, hospitals, schools, and communication systems were destroyed. The economic fallout of the war is seen in the fact that despite its vast resources, Angola today is one of the poorest African states. The dramatic fall in agricultural production during the war has led to widespread famine because Angolans are unable to feed themselves.

At the end of the war in 2002, Angola began a journey of national reconciliation and reconstruction. Since then, the nation has struggled with economic recovery and political reform. The enormous task of reconstruction has been aided by significant international humanitarian aid, especially in the health-care sector and food relief. Even before the end of the war, groups such as the International Medical Corps (IMC) and Doctors without Borders (DWB) had been very active in helping Angolans rebuild their collapsed health system and infrastructure. The IMC has continued to assist Angolans in the areas of maternal and child health care through programs of immunization and training of health-care personnel.

One of the most important challenges of postwar reconstruction is ridding the country of land mines buried during the war. The war saw all the various parties to the conflict—government forces, UNITA rebels, Cuban and South African troops—extensively use mines. According to estimates, about 20 million land mines remained spread throughout Angola's 18 provinces by the close of the conflict. Angola is said to have the worst problem with land mines in the world. The mines were buried haphazardly and indiscriminately without any form of mapping. Consequently, their removal has been costly, dangerous, slow, and tedious.

CULTURAL ISSUES

Despite the ravages of two long wars, Angola's rich and varied culture is preserved. Traditional and modern Euro-Christian Western values coexist and define the country's cultural character. In spite of modernization and

Westernization induced by colonialism and Christianization, ancient traditions persist. Precolonial political, social, and religious institutions are still very much a part of the Angolan culture, especially among rural dwellers.

The chief vehicle of the spread of Western culture in Angola is Christianity. Roman Catholicism is very strong, dating to the Portuguese proselytism in the area from the fifteenth century. More than the colonial regime, missionaries propagated Western education and values, but the spread of the new culture was not evenly distributed. Atlantic coastal areas and urban centers with strong and long-term Portuguese influence tended to be more assimilated into the new culture compared with rural and interior areas. For instance, Western values are predominant in port cities such as Luanda and Benguela, which have large European populations and long-term residence.

Largely because of centuries of the Atlantic slave trade through which a large number of Angolans were transported to the New World, elements of Angola's culture today are found there, especially in Brazil.

NOTES

1. Prendergast, *Angola's Deadly War*, 1.

2. Figures are drawn from *CIA World Factbook* (2006 edition), http://geography. about.com/library/cia/blcangola.htm.

3. "Angola Exports," *CIA World Factbook*.

4. "Trade with Angola: 2003," U.S. Census Bureau, Foreign Trade Division, Data Dissemination Branch (Washington, DC: 2003), http://www.census.gov/ foreign-trade/balance/c7620.html#2003.

5. "Angola Imports," *CIA World Factbook*.

6. See "World Military Expenditures and Arms Transfers, 1998," U.S. Arms Control and Disarmament Agency, http://www.globalsecurity.org/military/world/ spending.htm.

7. See "Bié."

8. "Angola External Debt," *CIA World Factbook*.

9. The constitution was revised on January 7, 1978; August 11, 1980; March 6, 1991; and August 26, 1992.

10. For the details of the election results, see "Elections in Angola," *African Elections Database*, http://africanelections.tripod.com/ao.html#1992_Presidential_Election.

11. For more about the Khoisan, see Barnard, *Hunters and Herders of Southern Africa*; Boonzaier, Malherbe, Smith, and Berens, *The Cape Herders*; and Steyn, *Vanished Lifestyles*.

12. Important studies of early Christianity in the Kongo are provided in Thornton, *Kongolese Saint Anthony*; Sweet, *Recreating Africa*; and John Thornton, "The Development of an African Catholic Church in the Kingdom of Kongo."

13. Studies of the demography of the Atlantic slave trade have put forth various figures. For more credible figures, see Lovejoy, *Transformations in Slavery,* 19, 46–62, 81, and 146; see also a critique of the demography in Inikori, "Africa and the Trans-Atlantic Slave Trade," 405–9.

14. Rodney, "European Activity and African Resistance in Angola," 63–64; and Wheeler and Pelissier, *Angola,* 171.

15. For a brief analysis of Portuguese colonial rule in Africa, see Falola, "Colonialism and Exploitation."

16. The Lusaka peace process is discussed in Human Rights Watch, *Angola Unravels.*

2

Religion and Worldview

IN PRACTICALLY EVERYTHING they do, the people of Angola are influenced by their religious outlook and their beliefs and ideas about life, human existence, and the universe. Indeed, religion and worldview play a central role in their day-to-day activities, perspectives, and decisions on current and future activities, interpersonal and group relations, and even the questions of life, death, and the aftermath. Indeed, individual and group identity, to a large extent, is defined by religion.

Angolans are a deeply religious people who, whether they practice Christianity, Islam, or forms of traditional religion, value and greatly respect religious events, rituals, and ceremonies. National religious holidays are observed, and religious festivities are quite popular and frequently celebrated.

The Angolan constitution expressly guarantees free expression of religious faith. It also prevents anyone from being discriminated against on the basis of religious affiliation, both in private or public settings. As a secular state governed by the doctrine of separation of church and state, officially the government and other political authorities in the country do not interfere in religion. All religious institutions are expected to be respected and treated equally, provided they act within the bounds of law and do not constitute a threat to national interest and security.

In reality, however, Angola has not always tolerated religious expression. Before the state abandoned Marxism and adopted free enterprise in 1991, the left-leaning Popular Movement for the Liberation of Angola (Movimento Popular de Libertação de Angola, MPLA) government held the traditional Marxist-Leninist view of religion as archaic and detrimental to state modernization. Christianity, Angola's main religion and a colonial bequeathal, was seen by the government as an instrument of Portuguese imperialism. Even though many of Angola's immediate postindependence rulers were products of parochial schools, their affiliation with Marxism precluded them from formal acknowledgment of or commitment to religion. The Marxist-Leninist government did not oppose the existence of religious institutions, although it did not officially endorse religion. In 1978, however, the government required that religious organizations, including churches, register to be legally recognized. In addition to the Roman Catholic Church, a number of Protestant churches were recognized, including the Baptist Convention of Angola, the Baptist Evangelical Church of Angola, the United Methodist Church, the Evangelical Church of Angola, the Congregational Evangelical Church of Angola, the Evangelical Church of South-West Angola, the Assemblies of God, the Seventh-Day Adventist Church, the Reformed Evangelical Church of Angola, and the Union of Evangelical Churches of Angola. For the establishment of new churches, the government required a permit.

The government's stringent measures were designed to ensure greater government control of religious institutions and to ensure that they towed the official state and party line. Groups such as the Jehovah's Witnesses and the Seventh-Day Adventists were for some time under the government's suspicious eyes. It was the African independent church Our Lord Jesus Christ Church in the World, however, that was accused of opposing the state that came under the heavy hand of the government. Perceived to be sympathetic to the National Union for the Total Independence of Angola (União Nacional para a Independência Total de Angola, UNITA), the church remained banned by the government through much of the 1970s and until 1988 when it was legally recognized. The meddling in religious affairs by the government prompted the Roman Catholic Church late in 1977 to publicly accuse the government of violation of freedom of religion.

The state's strict control of religion was relaxed in the late 1980s when religious leaders had not become, as expected, instruments of political opposition to the ruling MPLA. Less suspicious of religion and it role in national life, the government became more tolerant of religious institutions. Since the end of the civil war in April 2002, greater acceptance of religious freedom by the government has become more evident. In May 2004, the National Assembly further guaranteed the constitutional right of freedom of religion when it passed a law on freedom of conscience, worship, and religion. The law highlighted the right of the citizens to profess a religious faith or not to profess one. It also reinforced the unrestricted freedom of churches and other religious bodies to organize and practice their faiths within the limits of the law.[1]

CHRISTIANITY

Christianity is the dominant religion in Angola to which about 55 percent of the people adhere. Most Christians are Roman Catholics, whereas others belong to Protestant and evangelical denominations. Angola's coastal area in the west, a part of the prominent fifteenth-century Kongo Kingdom, was one of the earliest regions in Africa to receive Christianity. The religion was introduced to the kingdom by the Portuguese in 1491 when missionaries began to arrive there. By the end of the fifteenth century, the faith had become very popular. A principal pillar of the propagation of Christianity was an early sixteenth-century Manikongo (king), Nzinga Mbemba (1506–43), who converted to Christianity and became popularly known by his baptismal name, Afonso.[2] This Christian king was reputed to have built churches in the kingdom through the assistance of Portuguese Roman Catholic missionaries. Responsible for the early work of evangelism in Angola, Portuguese missionaries established educational institutions through which the African clergy was trained.

During his reign, Afonso I made Roman Catholicism a religion not only of the court but also of the state. Christianity further expanded under the reign of his son, Henrique, an ordained Roman Catholic bishop, the first African so elevated to that position. He discouraged traditional African religion

One of the many churches in the country. Courtesy of Armando J. Rodriguez, Jr.

and ordered the destruction of the paraphernalia of the worship of African traditional gods.

The initial Christian activities in Angola were centered on São Salvador, in the northern part of the country. During the early colonial period, Christianity was mainly propagated by Portuguese Roman Catholic missionaries. By the late nineteenth century, however, Protestant missionaries from the United States, Canada, and the United Kingdom joined mission work in Angola. African American mission organizations were particularly active in Angola, the Galangue mission in Huíla Province being an example.[3] An important instrument of proselytization was Western education. Although the colonial government was reluctant to provide Angolans education, the Christian missionaries championed it.[4]

Since the early 1990s, Angolan churches have experienced tremendous growth in terms of membership. This is true not only of the Roman Catholic Church but also of the Protestant and independent churches. With an annual growth rate of 5 percent,[5] church and other Christian organizations and institutions have become increasingly formidable parts of society with power to play a prominent role in the life of the country. They are engaged in civic education and humanitarian medical and social work in Angola. Some are also involved in the task of conflict resolution and reconciliation. They have been particularly active in the rural areas that are not easily accessible to government workers.

Perhaps, the most notable role of the church in Angola in the last quarter of a century is its increasingly vocal voice for social justice. In the late 1970s, some churches occasionally spoke for peace in the civil war. For instance, in September 1977, a thanksgiving service under the auspices of the Union of Churches of the Holy Spirit in Angola (UIESA) was held in Luanda and in other places to demand peace. From about the late 1980s, however, after the conflict had dragged on for years, churches increasingly called for peace. In November 1989, Roman Catholic bishops, in an open letter read in all the parishes, called on UNITA and the MPLA to end the civil war and hold free elections.

The frustration at the inability of the warring factions to make progress toward peace compelled Angolan churches, traditionally divided by ethnic cleavages, to mend their differences and mount a united front for peace. Thus, in a demonstration of unity, they came together to lend a strong and united voice to the popular call for peace. In September 1995, a meeting of Christian Churches in Angola (EDICEA) was held at the initiative of the Council of Christian Churches in Angola (CICA) and the Evangelicals Association in Angola (AEA). The meeting, which attracted about 400 participants, demanded a speedy implementation of the Lusaka Protocol by the government and UNITA. Also, a rally of the coalition of the Roman Catholic Church, CICA, and AEA at the Luanda National Stadium on July 14, 1998, brought together 40,000 Christians from different denominations in prayers for peace. CICA, which had been established in 1977, was no more merely an ecumenical institution but began to be very active in the peace drive.

The renewal of war in 1999 increased the sense of urgency within the church for a permanent cessation of the conflict. Therefore, the church increased pressure on the warring parties to negotiate peace. On a number of occasions, between 2000 and the end of the war in 2002, churches joined efforts through interdenominational organizations, conferences, prayers, worship services, peace campaigns, and marches to put pressure on the government and UNITA to end the war and start the process of national reconciliation.

Angolan churches have also become a formidable force in the campaign for the promotion of democracy and respect for human rights. This is despite the government's opposition to religious institutions playing a role in politics. In speaking out on issues of human rights, the churches have sometimes aligned themselves with civic groups. In January 1990, the Angolan Civic Association (ACA) was formed with close ties to the Roman Catholic Church. One of its major goals was respect for human rights by the warring parties.

The church has employed a variety of instruments such as seminars, worships, and conferences in its social campaign. For established churches like the Roman Catholic Church, the radio has been an effective tool in reaching the people. Through its broadcast station, Radio Ecclesia, the church has raised issues of civil rights and democracy. Programs on other pertinent issues like land mines, tolerance, and reconciliation have been produced. CICA and AEA also have used radio broadcasts for the same purpose. Apart from the radio, many churches have used magazines, newspapers, and newsletters for their campaigns on social issues. The Roman Catholic Church, for instance, used its monthly newspaper, *Apostalado,* to call for the cessation of hostilities during the war. With the increasing access to the Internet, a few churches such as the Roman Catholics have also created Web sites to reach the larger community.

Commitment to social issues does not mean that Angolan churches have laid aside their primary ecumenical responsibility. Worship services on Sundays and often midweek are always well attended. Irrespective of denomination, church services are mainly conducted in Portuguese and in the local languages. In major cities with appreciable foreign population such as Luanda, Huambo, Lobito, and Benguela, however, interdenominational church services conducted in English are common. Since the end of the civil war, outdoor crusades, sometimes in stadiums, have brought thousands of people together in worship and prayer. Radio broadcasts of church services and other religious programs have become popular as well.

Roman Catholicism

Christians in Angola belong predominantly to the Roman Catholic Church in Angola (Igreja Catolica em Angola, ICA). This is a reflection of colonial history in which the Portuguese colonialists were mainly Roman Catholics. Angola has 3 archdioceses, located in Huambo, Luanda, and Lubango, and 12 dioceses. Numbering almost 5 million and constituting about 44.14 percent of the population according to a 2005 estimate,[6] Roman Catholics have their highest numbers in the densely populated coastal west, particularly among the Bakongo in Cabinda and among the Mbundu of Luanda and Cuanza Norte Provinces. This concentration of Roman Catholics among western coastal groups could be attributed to their long colonial interaction with the Portuguese. Further inland among the Ovimbundu, predominant in Benguela and Huambo Provinces, Roman Catholicism is less strong. Groups in the eastern and southern provinces tend even less to be Roman Catholics.[7]

Since the colonial period, the Roman Catholic Church has played a large role in the provision of Western education to the people of Angola. Before the early 1960s, the source of education for Africans was almost exclusively the Roman Catholic missions. Today, many elementary and secondary schools are managed by the church, and education is mainly provided in Portuguese. Although Roman Catholic influence in higher education is marginal, the church supports the Catholic University of Angola in Luanda, one of the universities in the country established in 1999.

Protestants and Evangelicals

The English Baptist Church was the first Protestant organization to establish a mission in Angola when in 1878 it founded a mission in São Salvador (now M'banza Kongo) among the Bakongo. Other Protestant missions from other parts of Europe, the United States, and Canada followed suit in different areas of Angola.

In the past, particularly during the colonial period, Protestant activities were frowned upon in Angola, and this severely prohibited the growth of Protestantism. A steady rise of Protestant and evangelical denominations has occurred in the last few years, however. Protestants today constitute an estimated 20 percent of the population.[8] Some of the fastest growing denominations are the Evangelical Reformed churches, the Baptist Mission, the Assemblies of God, the Seventh-Day Adventists, the Presbyterian Church, the

Worshippers in a Luanda church. Christianity is the most popular religion in Angola and many people belong to the Roman Catholic Church. There are other protestant and evangelical denominations. Courtesy of Armando J. Rodriguez, Jr.

Church of Christ, the Congregationalist Church, and the various Pentecostal evangelical churches, which are rapidly becoming more popular all over sub-Saharan Africa.

Unlike orthodox denominations like the Roman Catholic Church, the Protestant and evangelical missions adopt a more aggressive proselytization. Their missionaries have traditionally combined evangelism with the provision of social services such as medical care. During the colonial period, Protestant missionaries made conscious efforts to penetrate the cultures of the local people by having at least a working knowledge of their languages and by providing them medical and welfare services. In the contemporary period, Protestant and evangelical denominations seem to have succeeded better than their Roman Catholic counterparts in grassroots efforts. Their clergy continue to be more involved with the community both in religious matters and in welfare assistance. Following are some of the major evangelical and Protestant churches:

1. Evangelical Congregational Church in Angola (Igreja Evangelica Congrgacional em Angola, IECA).
2. Evangelical Pentecostal Church of Angola (Missao Evangelica Pentecostal de Angola, MEPA).

3. United Evangelical Church of Angola (Igreja Evangelica Unida de Angola, IEUGA).

4. Evangelical Baptist Church of Angola (Igreja Evangelica Baptista de Angola, IEBA).

5. Evangelical Church of the Apostles of Jerusalem.

6. Evangelical Reformed Church of Angola (Igreja Evangelica Reformada de Angola, IERA).

7. United Methodist Church of Angola (Igreja Metodista Unida de Angola, IMUA).

8. Presbyterian Church in Angola (Igreja Presbiteriana de Angola, IPA).

9. Seventh-Day Adventist Church (Igreja Adventista do Stimo Dia, IASD).

10. Lutheran Church of Angola (Igreja Luterana de Angola).

Although many of the Protestant and evangelical churches have histories that date to the late nineteenth century, new ones continue to be established. For instance, the Independent Presbyterian Church in Angola (Igreja Presbiteriana Independente em Angola, IPIA) came into being only in 1991 when it was formed by Angolan refugees returning from the Democratic Republic of the Congo (DRC). Some of the new churches are offshoots of established ones. The Independent Reformed Church in Angola (Igreja Reformada Independente em Angola, IRIA) emerged from IERA in 1996, whereas the Christian Presbyterian Church of Angola (Igreja Crista Presbiteriana da Angola, ICPA), formed in 1998, had its roots in IERA and IPA. Likewise, the Reformed Church of Angola (Igreja Reformada de Angola, IRA) and the Biblical Christian Church in Angola (Igreja Biblica Crista em Angola, IBCA), both of which started in 2000, took their roots from IERA.

Independent African Churches

Independent African churches are those exclusively established by African Christians as opposed to the mainstream European-pioneered mission churches.[9] They are often established by a charismatic leader who, more often than not, originally belonged to a mission church. The indigenous churches, therefore, begin as a breakaway faction of the European-established mission churches.

A number of independent churches thrive in Angola, and they are broadly of three types. The first type, the Kimbangui churches, emerged out of protests by Africans to the mission churches' opposition to aspects of African traditional practices such as polygamy, puberty rites, and marriage customs. Perhaps the most prominent of such churches is Our Lord Jesus Christ Church in the World (Igreja do Nosso Senhor Jesus Cristo no Mundo). This church was established in 1849 by Simon Mtoko (Simão Toco), a charismatic figure from Uíge Province who tailored his sect along the lines of the Kimbangui movement popular in central and southern Africa.[10] The Kimbanguist Church is an indigenous sect founded in the Belgian Congo (now the DRC) in the early 1920s by a prophet, Simon Kimbangui, who was formerly a Baptist adherent. The Mtokoists, as members of the Angolan Our Lord Jesus Christ Church in the World are popularly called, believe in incorporating elements of African tradition and cultural practices into the Christian religion.

The Kimbangui Church (Igreja Kimbanguista em Angola) is another Kimbanguist faith in Angola. Although it is not formally affiliated with the original Congolese church, its adherents adopt the Kimbanguist articles of faith. Other churches along the lines of the Kimbanguist movement, although less popular, also exist. They include the Church of Lassy Zepherin (Igreja de Lassy Zepherin), popular among the Bakongo in Cabinda; the Holy Spirit Group (Grupo do Espirito Santo); and the Black Church (Igreja dos Negros), a prototype of the original Congolese church founded by Simon Mpadi, a former Baptist catechist who turned Kimbanguist.

The second type of independent African churches is made up of charismatic, Holy Ghost ministries that claim superior spirituality than other churches. More than the Kimbanguists, the Pentecostals have made a radical departure from the patterns of orthodox Christianity and liberal Protestantism in doctrinal matters and worship. Instead of the solemn, reverent worship of the mission churches, the Pentecostal churches employ an informal worship that involves ecstatic singing and clapping of hands, dancing, loud prayers, and the manifestation of the Holy Spirit expressed through speaking in tongues. Aside from the informal worship, the Pentecostals interpret the Bible literally and believe in prophesies, miracles through prayer, and faith healing. To them, holiness is central to Christian living, and they expect their adherents to be filled with the Holy Spirit to live a victorious, sanctified life. Thus, members are enjoined to refrain from any practices considered sinful, such as alcohol consumption, adultery and fornication, cigarette smoking, and gambling.

Also, although the Kimbanguists incorporate aspects of African social, cultural, and religious beliefs into the practice of Christianity, the Pentecostal churches see such traditional beliefs as evil, demonic, and incompatible with the Christian faith. They thus oppose their members participating in traditional festivals, ceremonies, and rituals. The Western mode of dressing is encouraged, especially among the clergy.

A few churches fit in between the two categories of independent African churches discussed previously. Unlike the Kimbanguists, they do not subscribe to the overt infusion of African tradition into Christianity. They also are not considered as spiritual as the charismatic, Pentecostal churches. An example of such a church is the African Apostolic Church in Angola (Igreja Apostolica Africana em Angola).

Foreign Mission Activities

Angola's long and destructive civil war has made the country a fertile ground for foreign mission activities. To be sure, foreign missions have always played an important role in the historical development of Christianity in Angola. The devastation that attended the civil war and the enormous task of post-war reconstruction, however, ensure that the financially strapped Angolan government relies heavily on nongovernmental organizations, including religious institutions.

Overseas missions active in Angola include a variety of Christian denominations; most are U.S. and Europe-based, like the American Methodist Episcopal Church and the Baptist Missionary Society (BMS), respectively. The missions generally believe that the propagation of the Gospel is one of the ways by which the deep wounds of the civil war may be healed. Thus, as proselytization is primary in their agenda, they seek to serve the spiritual needs of Angolans through evangelism, church establishment, and clergy training. Grants also have been provided to pastors to enable them to do mission work in rural places.

Foreign missions are concerned not only with the spiritual nourishment of Angolans, however; they are also active in humanitarian work to raise the quality of life, especially in badly depressed areas. They provide health education and medical services to villagers to combat a variety of illnesses and diseases such as tuberculosis, typhoid, and malaria. Some have instituted food aid programs, helped build schools, and catered to children orphaned by the war or abandoned by parents. Generally, these missions have invested time and money in Angola to raise the living standard of the people.

Since the end of the civil war, various foreign-based religious organizations have become operative in Angola. For instance the American Leprosy Mission (ALM), whose work in the country dates to the post–World War II period, is involved in leprosy control through the provision of medical assistance and supplies and the training of leprosy workers. The United Kingdom–based BMS World Mission is another popular foreign mission.

Some of the foreign missions are based in the major cities, whereas others work in rural settings. In most cases, they operate in conjunction with local churches and religious institutions. For instance, the ALM, which operates in Benguela, Huíla, Namibe, and Huambo Provinces, is affiliated with some of Angola's largest evangelical churches, especially, the Evangelical Congregational Church in Angola (IECA). The World Mission of the BMS works with Angola's Evangelical Baptist Church (IEBA) to provide educational benefits and health services and relief to people in impoverished areas. Particularly, the BMS has been active in combating tuberculosis in Angola and has established TB clinics and health centers in Luanda and other cities and has provided nurses.[11]

Religion and War

Angola's protracted and devastating civil war has had adverse repercussions on the church, as it has had on virtually every aspect of national life. The church suffered a great many losses, both material and human, during the war. It lost congregation members to death and dislocation; it lost buildings and other infrastructure to wanton destruction. Although the church was deeply scarred by the war, its perseverance ensured its survival. Indeed, the end of the war and the need for rebuilding has provided new opportunities for cooperation among the various Christian dominations. The commitment to cooperate in the face of the enormous challenges of postwar reconstruction has transcended ethnic and political divisions that have been the bane of the church. Thus, since the end of the war, various denominations have pooled resources at their disposal in the areas of education, health, aid relief, and reconciliation for the betterment of the society. The Luanda-based CICA has been instrumental throughout the nation in assisting churches to provide various types of rural community developmental services.

INDIGENOUS RELIGIONS AND WORLDVIEW

An estimated 47 percent of the Angolan population, especially in the rural areas, still practices various forms of indigenous religions.[12] Even for many people who profess Christianity and lay claim to membership in Christian denominations, their Christian faith does not preclude them from identifying with aspects of traditional religious practices and beliefs. Also, it is not uncommon to find Western-educated people in urban areas consult traditional priests.

There are as many indigenous religions as there are ethnic groups or subgroups in Angola. Usually, ethnic groups, subgroups, lineages, and even families identify with particular traditional religions although related groups often share specific elements of religious beliefs and practices. Generally, each religion has its own set of beliefs, values, rituals, and worship systems. They often share some common features, however, such as the belief in a supreme deity identified by various names according to the ethnolinguistic group.

The Supreme Being

The supreme deity in the cosmology of many Angolan groups is the god of creation. Known as Kalunga among the Chokwe and Nzambi among the BaKongo, the supreme god is not only credited with the creation of the universe and everything in it, he is also imbued with supreme power over the affairs of men on earth. Among certain groups, the supreme being is considered so powerful that he cannot be approached by mortals. The BaKongo, for instance, according to an account, regard Nzambi as the "sovereign master" who is "unapproachable" and "inaccessible." Thus, "they render him no worship, for he has need of none."[13]

Some groups believe that even though the supreme deity is powerful, with life-and-death power over his creation, they still believe he can be approached, normally through worship and sacrifices. The avenue of approach may be indirect, however, through lower or lesser gods.

Ancestral Spirit Worship

Traditional religion in Angola is more than religious belief systems and practices. Like other religions, forms of indigenous religions constitute a way of life and the gateway through which their adherents view their world. As in most parts of sub-Saharan Africa, Angolans believe in life after death, and their indigenous religions recognize the universe as a unified entity with the living very much in close connection with the spirits of dead ancestors (*mahamba,* among the Chokwe). Ancestors are believed to be capable of playing a part in the lives of the living, and thus the spirit of a dead family member or of a prominent member of the community or ethnic group can be worshipped. Indeed, ancestral worship is a common denominator for many of the traditional religions.

The worship of ancestors is important and, in fact, considered mandatory among many groups. To neglect to do it is to jeopardize the welfare of an individual or of the society at large and even of the descent group. To honor the spirit of the ancestors by worship is thus necessary to curry their favor or to appease them so that they may avert impending disasters such as famines, plagues, diseases, personal losses, and other catastrophes. Ancestral worship is conducted in the form of ritual performances and ceremonies usually involving sacrifices, often of animals.

Closely related to the ancestral spirit is a belief in nature spirits. Many Angolan traditional religionists indulge in the worship of spirits residing in natural entities and landscapes such as rocks, trees, sky, sun, and thunder and lightning.

Evil Spirits and Divination

Angolans also very much believe in the existence of evil spirits that are at the root of individual or collective misfortunes. They believe that there are sorcerers (*wanga* among the Chokwe) who are capable of commanding evil spirits to inflict misfortunes on others. Thus, an individual who encounters illness can quickly blame it on the sorcerer, who invariably is a jealous neighbor, coworker, acquaintance, or some spiteful or malevolent individual. Apart from sorcerers, witches (*feiticeiros*) are also believed to exist, and the practice of witchcraft (*feiticismo*) is not uncommon.

In a society in which sorcery and witchcraft are widely believed, the diviner, called *kimbanda* (*nganga,* among the Kongo), assumes a position of importance because of his or her power not only to communicate with the world of spirits but also the ability to exorcise evil spirits. Most diviners are trained, but some claim hereditary spiritual power of divination. The diviner can thus detect the spirit responsible for an illness and effect the healing of the inflicted. Among the Chokwe, basket divination is popular in which the diviner deciphers the cause of an illness through the tossing of divination objects inside a basket. Once the illness is diagnosed and its cause determined, which might be the machinations of a sorcerer or the failure to perform necessary sacrifices to some gods or spirits, a treatment is then prescribed by the diviner, which might involve a medicine concoction to specific sacrifices. All this is done for a fee, but reputation and proficiency attract patronage and higher prices. Some diviners deal with specific cases, whereas others are generalists. Fake diviners are not unknown.

ISLAM

The advent of the Portuguese on the Angolan coast in the late fifteenth century and their ecumenical enterprises thereafter ensured that the region would be predominantly Christian. The Kongo Kingdom, a part of which encompassed northern Angola, existed as a Christian kingdom for centuries. Given this scenario, Islam did not emerge as a significant religion in Angola. Possible Islamic influence from the Swahili coast of eastern Africa did not materialize, and Angola has been a predominantly Christian nation. Islam is very much a religion of the minority, and Muslims constitute only 1 to 2.5 percent of the population.

In the last few years, however, the Muslim community in Angola has grown appreciably and Islamic activities have become more common in major cities. Mosques have sprung up in a number of places and Quranic schools have been built to provide Islamic instructions and teach Arabic language to adherents. The Muslim community is predominantly made up of foreigners, especially businessmen and migrants from western Africa and southwest Asia. Some Angolans have converted to Islam as a result of active proselytization by Muslim organizations such as the Associacao Islamica de Desenvolvimento de Angola (Association of the Development of Islam in Angola, AIDA). Other Angolans had come in contact with Islam while refugees in neighboring states with a strong Islamic presence. Some Angolans have adopted the Islamic way of dressing. This is particularly true of women who converted to Islam by way of marriage to Muslim men.

Muslim affairs are generally governed by the Supreme Council of Angolan Muslims, based in Luanda.

Other Religions

A tiny portion of the Angolan population, again mainly foreigners, practices other forms of religion. In the Asian community, Hinduism is practiced. Synagogues in urban areas also serve the interests of the Jewish community. Greek Orthodox churches also exist.

THE LEGACY OF RELIGION

Religion in Angola has an enduring legacy and continues to play an important role in the life of the country. Christianity is well established and thrives further, not only in urban settings but also in rural areas. The postwar reconstruction effort has provided Christian churches and foreign missions opportunities for evangelization. The Pentecostal denominations, with their emphasis on spirituality, are particularly active in the spread of the Gospel. Christian churches also have greatly increased their reach beyond religious issues. They constitute a formidable part of the Angolan social movement for peace, justice, and democracy.

The predominance of Christianity has threatened indigenous religions in a number of ways. First, many Christian denominations, most especially the Pentecostal churches, condemn many aspects of traditional culture. Second, Western education, to which Christianity has always been identified, is incompatible with many traditional beliefs, particularly the explanation of phenomena like evil spirits as the cause of sickness or natural disaster. Last, indigenous religions lack the capital to effectively establish on a national level like the churches. Despite all these threats, indigenous religions are still very much part of Angolan religiocultural reality because they are deeply rooted in the historical development of the people who have practiced them for centuries.

In Angola, the various religious groups coexist peacefully, unlike in some African states like Nigeria and Sudan, which are bedeviled with religious conflict. This is not to say, however, that there had not been some tensions between Muslims and non-Muslims.

NOTES

1. For details about this law, see "Parliament Passes Law."

2. For early Christianity in the Kongo Kingdom, see Isichei, *A History of Christianity in Africa;* Hilton, *The Kingdom of Kongo;* Jordán, *The Kongo Kingdom;* and Mann, *West Central Africa.*

3. See Henderson, *Galangue.* For other early African American mission activities, see Labode, "'A Native Knows a Native.'" For the general history of U.S. Protestant missions in Angola, see Soremekun, "A History of the American Board Mission in Angola."

4. For more discussions on this, see Isichei, *A History of Christianity in Africa;* and Bauer, *2000 Years of Christianity in Africa.*

5. World Vision UK, "Angola."

6. Wikipedia, "Roman Catholicism by Country."

7. Thornton, "The Development of an African Catholic Church," 147–67. For statistics on the Catholic strength in the provinces, see Cheney, "Angola Statistics by Province by Name."

8. Recent estimate as cited in "Angola" in Ember and Ember, *Countries and Their Cultures,* 59.

9. Independent African churches as related to South Africa are discussed in Pretorius and Jafta, "A Branch Springs Out," 211–26.

10. For more on Simon Mtoko, see Grenfell, "Simão Toco," 210–26.

11. For more information about BMS World Mission, see http://www.bmsworldmission.org.

12. Central Intelligence Agency, "Angola."

13. Van Joseph Wing, *Études Bakongo: Sociologie, Religion et Magie.* Translation is in Smith, *African Ideas of God,* 159.

3

Literature and Media

ANGOLANS HAVE CONTRIBUTED significantly to the growing Portuguese literature in Africa. This is in spite of the country's long and brutal war of independence and an equally prolonged and devastating postindependence civil war, both of which virtually destroyed the cultural infrastructure. Although literary production did not cease altogether during the war years, the end of the civil war in 2002 and the return to peace have brought renewed vigor to the literary sector. The Angola government has prioritized cultural renewal and development as part of the national recovery effort. In February 2005, the Ministry of Culture inaugurated a commission of 14 specialists to produce a history of Angolan literature.[1] Today, Angola is a leader in Lusophone African literature and has an extensive literary output.

The media services in Angola consist of the print (newspapers and magazines) and electronic (radio, television, and Internet). The media have not faired very well, and what could have been a vibrant press made up of government-owned and private media organizations has consistently been stifled. Since the colonial period, the practice of journalism has been conducted under an oppressive atmosphere. In independent Angola, even though the constitution expressly guarantees freedom of expression and explicitly forbids press censorship, the state has suppressed freedom of expression and intimidated journalists through detention without trial, unwarranted jailing, and even murdering media personnel.

The end of the civil war provided Angola the opportunity to begin to build a truly independent press. Indeed, some level of progress may have been made along this line. In August 2005, the government approved a new press law that, according to the deputy minister of mass media, Manuel Miguel de

Carvalho, "is a more modern and democratic consensual tool."[2] It is much too early, however, to determine the extent to which reforms will be truly implemented in the mass media sector.

LITERATURE

Angola's leading position in the literature of Lusophone Africa is a reflection of the country's rich cultural tradition, which has withstood years of devastating wars. The people of Angola are rich in various forms of oral literature, including poetic renditions, folk stories, and ritual dramas. Modern Angolan literature, however, is reflected in the different genres of literature in Portuguese: fiction, poetry, and drama.

One of the legacies of Western education is the emergence of a class of intellectuals and writers whose primary avenue of literary discourse is Portuguese. Although some literature has been produced in indigenous languages, Angola's literary tradition basically has flourished in Portuguese. Some of the most prominent Angolan writers are those whose works have been produced in Portuguese, and many of these works were published in Portugal. Increasingly, Angolan creative works are being translated into other languages, especially English and French. This has given the country's major writers, such as novelist Arturo Carlos Maurício Pestana dos Santos (also known as Pepetela), and others exposure beyond the Lusophone world. A number of them have had their works published in the prestigious African Writers Series, which has been dominated by Anglophone writers.[3]

Modern Angolan literature has been defined by three principal historical realities: colonialism, nationalism, and civil war. The legacies of the particularly severe form of Portuguese colonialism, the anticolonial struggle in the form of a guerrilla war, and the protracted civil war are critical to the understanding of the development of Lusophone Angolan literature and continue to inform literary works in the country.

PRECOLONIAL LITERATURE

Except in a few areas, most of precolonial Africa, including Angola, lacked a tradition of written literature. Thus, the literature of Angola before the region's contact with Europeans was primarily oral, appreciated through recitation. Although largely unwritten, oral literature possesses the same forms present in modern literature, namely prose, verse, and drama. If modern literature is meant to educate, instruct, inform, and entertain, traditional literature exhibited the same utilitarian values. Unlike modern literature, however, the oral genre lacked textual preservation because it was not scripted.

Nonetheless, oral tradition was preserved through memory and transmitted by word of mouth from one generation to another.

Myths, Legends, and Folktales

Prose in precolonial Angolan literature was primarily in the form of myths, legends, and folktales. Though they vary from culture to culture in terms of content, they essentially perform the same functions. Through mythical stories, Angolans sought to provide rational explanation to the riddle of creation, particularly of the universe and its constitution. Myths also recount stories of foundation and development of societies, communities, lineages, clans, and ethnic groups.

Legends are closely related to myths, but they are mainly avenues of recounting heroic deeds of important historical figures who are often credited with extraordinary and larger-than-life deeds. An Mbundu legend, "King Kitamba kia Xhiba,"[4] relates the heroic deeds of a *kimbanda,* a diviner or traditional healer. According to this legend, Kitamba, a noted chief, lost his beloved wife, Queen Muhongo. He embarked on endless days of mourning, refusing to eat or speak until his wife could be restored to life. By his order, his subjects joined him in mourning:

No man shall do anything. … The young people shall not shout; the women shall not pound; no one shall speak in the village.

As efforts to comfort Kitamba failed, his headmen summoned the *kimbanda,* who agreed to visit Kalunga, the land of the dead, to bring Queen Muhongo back to life. The *kimbanda* made preparations for his heroic journey:

He … directed some men to "dig a grave in my guest-hut at the fireplace," which they did, and he entered it with his little boy, giving two last instructions to his wife: to leave off her girdle [to dress negligently, as if in mourning] and to pour water every day on the fireplace. Then the men filled in the grave. The doctor saw a road open before him; he walked along it with his boy till he came to a village, where he found Queen Muhongo sitting, sewing a basket.

After locating the queen in the land of the dead, the *kimbanda* divulged the purpose of his errand:

Thou thyself, I have sought thee. Since thou art dead, King Kitamba will not eat, will not drink, will not speak. In the village they pound not; they speak not; he says, "If I shall talk, if I eat, go ye and fetch my head-wife." That is what brought me here. I have spoken.

The queen could not return though, for "here in Kalunga, never comes one … to return again." In any case, her husband would very soon join her in

Kalunga, the legend states. The *kimbanda* finally found his way back to earth after the queen had presented him the armlet buried with her, a testimony to his having truly visited the land of the dead. His return to earth was as dramatic as the whole journey itself:

Meanwhile, the doctor's wife had kept pouring water on the grave. One day she saw the earth beginning to crack; the cracks opened wider, and, finally, her husband's head appeared. He gradually made his way out, and pulled his small-son up after him.

Needless to say, the king died a few years thereafter to meet his beloved queen.

Although Angolans are inclined to taking mythical stories and legends as factual despite their obvious supernatural attributes, folktales are recognized as fictional. Although humans sometimes feature in these tales, as common to many African folktales, those from Angola also generally feature animals as main characters, sometimes cast as tricksters. At times, folktales may be an avenue to deliver moral instructions, but primarily they are intended to entertain and are thus often accompanied by songs and audience participation. An example of a typical Angolan folktale is one popular among the Mbaka of the northwestern part of the country. It is the tale of the frog who married a Sky Maiden through its ability to be cunning.[5] In this tale, a young man, Kimana (or Kimanaueze), wished to marry the Sky Maiden, and for this purpose he wrote a letter to her father, the Sun Chief. The question was how Kimana would deliver his letter proposing marriage to the Sky Maiden:

Kimana went to Rabbit. "Will you take this letter?"
Rabbit said, "I cannot go to Heaven."
Kimana went to Antelope. "Will you take this letter?"
Antelope said, "I cannot go to Heaven."
Kimana went to Hawk. "Will you take this letter?"
Hawk said, "I can go halfway. But I cannot go to Heaven."
Then Frog came to Kimana. "Why do you not take the letter yourself?"
Kimana said, "This I cannot do."
Frog said, "Then I will take it for you."
Kimana laughed. "Can a frog take a letter to Heaven?"
Frog said, "Whatever it is, I can do it. But only if I try."

As typical of animal characters in folktales, through trickery the frog successfully delivered Kimana's letter to the Sky Maiden. At the end of the story, the maiden was so impressed with the frog's cleverness that she chose to marry him instead of Kimana.

Proverbs and Riddles

Precolonial literature in poetry form included proverbs and riddles. Generally in African societies, a proverb is an important part of speech. Often very brief, a sentence or two, proverbs are abstract sayings that serve the primary purpose of adding explanation or analogy to a serious discourse. Although they do not provide direct meanings and the hearer is expected to deduce the intended meaning, proverbs add richness to conversations. Anyone adept in the use of proverbs is considered a person of wisdom and knowledge. Proverbs are sometimes also intended to convey humor.

Some Angolan proverbs have historical foundation, derived from the experiences of the people, particularly slavery and colonialism. An Umbundu proverb goes thus:

Ame olohaku hu onjekela; ko Ndombe si endi love.
Take or reject the advice as you please. You are the one that will be carried into servitude.[6]

This proverb is advice against a desire that will likely have an adverse repercussion. The proverb's foundation can be traced to the European slave trade of the fifteenth century that sent a great number of Angolans into captivity.

Riddles are similar to proverbs in that they are both based on societal experiences and conveyed in poetic form. Unlike proverbs, however, riddles are primarily intended for entertainment but also task the thought processes. The riddle, or what may be called a puzzle, is shrouded in obscure language but with hints. The riddle may be about anything, from people to plants and animals to objects. The presenter is often an elderly person, and the audience is primarily children or young people who are expected to untie the knot hidden in the riddle. Both proverbs and riddles are a vehicle by which the community's codes of conduct and behavior are conveyed.

Songs

Oral poetry in Angola is almost always in the form of songs, sung rather than spoken. Ritual performances during social and religious festivals and during ceremonies such as coronations or installations of chiefs, child namings, marriages, and burials are often accompanied by performance of special songs. Praise songs also may be rendered in praise of towns, clans, and lineages; deities and gods; and individuals, especially prominent people in the society such as chiefs and war heroes. Many ritual songs are epic poems.

COLONIAL LITERATURE

Written literature in Angola emerged with the arrival of Europeans and the introduction of Western education by mission schools. The colonial period produced intellectuals, initially mainly *mestiços,* and later black Angolans, who contributed to the development of colonial literature expressed in Portuguese and based on Western values.

Colonial literature in Angola was initially practically monopolized by whites of Portuguese origin. Much of the work of colonial writers was racist in nature and intended to promote Portuguese culture. The colonial regime, especially under António Salazar's Estado Novo dictatorship, encouraged an exotic colonial literature in Angola. A few white Angolan writers, however, deviated from the preoccupation of Eurocentric colonial literature. An example was the novelist Fernando Monteiro de Castro Soromenho, one of the earliest Angolan writers often referred to as the "father of the Angolan novel" and once described as an "enlightened colonial writer."[7] Soromenho was born in Mozambique, and his work was a biting critique of the colonial system in Angola. He writings also focused on the life of the peoples of Angola and interracial relations. His works include three major novels, *Terra Morta* (*Dead Land,* 1949), *Viragem* (*Turning Point,* 1957), and *A Chaga* (*The Wound,* 1975).[8]

Despite the predominance of colonial writers, an indigenous written literature developed in Angola. Playing an important role in the emergence of what might also be regarded as national literature was the *mestiços* intellectual class, prominent particularly in Luanda and in other major coastal cities. *Mestiços* were more numerous in colonial Angola than in other Lusophone African colonies. There they constituted a powerful cultural force. Over the years when Luanda emerged as the administrative capital of Angola and the main cultural and literary center, the *mestiços* community of intellectuals began to write literature focused on Angolan culture.

The early twentieth century began to produce black Angolan writers who further advanced national literature. The preoccupation of these writers was to incorporate traditional literary elements into their works. The late arrival of black Angolan writers onto the literary scene was due primarily to the nature of the colonial system. First, Portuguese colonial educational policy discouraged the education of Africans and so retarded the emergence and growth of a black intellectual class. Second, the colonial system was detrimental to the flourishing of African literature. A severe form of press and literary censorship was particularly in vogue during the Estado Novo regime. A number of writers, including José Mena Abrantes, had to live in exile due to political harassment. Even white writers such as Soromenho and Luandino

Vieira, who attempted to produce authentic African literature, incurred the wrath of the colonial government. When Vieira's book *Luuanda* (1964), which is critical of the oppressive colonial system, won the Portuguese Writers' Society's Grand Prize for Fiction, a prestigious literary prize, in 1965, it was promptly banned by the colonial regime.

The nationalist struggle that began in earnest in the 1950s contributed a new dimension to Angolan national literature. New writers produced poetry and fiction that critiqued the prevailing social, economic, and political reality under the colonial system, issues that had been neglected by earlier generations of writers. Many of the new writers shared the revolutionary ideology generated by the anticolonial struggle, and this was very much reflected in their works. Indeed, a number of these writers were active in the nationalist movement. Agostinho Neto, one of the finest poets of modern Angola, was a leading figure in the anticolonial struggle from the 1940s. He was the leader of the Popular Movement for the Liberation of Angola (Movimento Popular de Libertação de Angola, MPLA) who became the first president of the country in 1975. Pepetela was also a guerrilla fighter in the MPLA and had fought in the Cabinda enclave in the war of independence. Vieira was also active in the struggle and, indeed, had been a political prisoner of the colonial regime in the 1960s because of his anticolonial activities. A number of the revolutionary writers were to play an important role in the politics of postcolonial Angola. Apart from Neto, who became the president, Pepetela served as the education minister under the MPLA government. Noted writer Uanhenga Xitu was also a health minister in the same government. Nevertheless, writers who were active in the anticolonial struggle but who participated in the postcolonial government have been severely criticized by self-exiled fellow writer Manuel dos Santos Lima:

In Angola, the overwhelming majority of writers are messianic, writers of annunciation. Those who participated in the liberation struggle have, after independence, aligned themselves with the government. I made the opposite choice, that is to remain faithful to the democratic ideals of my youth. This is why I live in exile.[9]

The violent anticolonial struggle led to the emergence of a large body of political and combative nationalist literature. Quite a number of writers produced some of their best works during the war of independence. Typical of the revolutionary literature of the nationalist era is Vieira's *A Vida Verdadeira de Domingos Xavier* (*The Real Life of Domingos Xavier*, 1974), an overtly political book that marked a departure from his earlier writings. Also important is Pepetela's reflections on the anticolonial struggle in *Mayombe* (1980), a novel based on tensions within a Marxist guerrilla force fighting against the Portuguese in the Mayombe Forest of Cabinda. The repressive condition of the late colonial period, however, drove the Angolan literary production underground.

Apart from creating a literature of resistance, the anticolonial period also produced writings that aimed to depict a more positive image of Angola than that portrayed by prejudiced colonial writers. Writers such as Agostinho Neto, Vieira, Xitu, Óscar Ribas, Arnaldo Santos, Lara Filho, and Mario Antonio helped promote an authentic national literature that would define a new and independent Angola. Optimism about a new nation with its own national identity and prospects for progress pervaded the works of these writers.

POSTCOLONIAL LITERATURE

The Africanization of Lusophone literature in Angola continued in the postcolonial period. Angolan writers, although still mainly using the Portuguese language as the avenue of expression, continued to consolidate an authentic Angolan literature that reflected the cultures and traditions of the land. Writers such as Agostinho Neto and Henrique Abranches helped fashion this *cultura nacional* through their works.

In terms of content, Angola's colonial history and the brutal war of independence that followed continued to inform literary works. In 1984, Pepetela published a fascinating work of fiction titled *Yaka,* essentially a literary excursion into Angola's history from colonialism through the period of the nationalist struggle. In the novel, Pepetela explores through the life of his main character, Alexandre Semedo, the major historical elements in the making of the Angolan state, namely the arrival of Portuguese immigrants in Angola, personified in Semedo's father, a convicted murderer deported from Portugal; the intersection of white and black Angola; Portuguese cultural hegemony; and the nationalist struggle. Other prominent postcolonial writers such as Vieira, Xitu, and Manuel Rui Alves Monteiro also have explored the themes of Portuguese colonialism and the violent anticolonial struggle.

For some writers, postcolonial literature focused on the prevailing state of political, social, and economic affairs in the new Angolan nation, particularly in the light of the prolonged and violent civil war. If nationalist literature expressed optimism in nationhood and nation building in Angola, this euphoria was dampened by the devastating civil war. An emerging theme in postcolonial writings was thus the abysmal failure of the postindependence state to manage ethnic, class, and ideological divisions and its inability to transform the society into a peaceful, progressive, and democratic one.

The disappointment of postindependence Angola featured prominently in modern Angolan literature. Many writers, Pepetela, for instance, turned to the questions of corruption, nepotism, and other social ills that plagued postindependence Angola. Pepetela's *O Desejo de Kianda* (*The Return of the Water Spirit,* 1995) is a biting critique of the modern-day Angolan elite for its failure to consolidate the gains of independence. In critiquing modern Angola, writers helped to raise the nation's consciousness regarding the direction in which it was headed.

A number of fiction writers experimented with historical novels set in precolonial times. For instance, in *Nzinga Mbandi* (1975), Manuel Pedro Pacavira fictionalized the historical character of Queen Mbandi, one of the famous political figures in precolonial Angolan history. Another historical novel is Pepetela's *Lueji* (1991), which in part is about another famous historical character, Lueji, queen of the Chokwe. Pepetela tells the story of the emergence of the state of Lunda through the life of Lueji.

CONTEMPORARY LITERATURE

In modern-day Angola, traditional literature has not died out but, indeed, continues to flourish despite the intellectual transformations that Western education has brought. Particularly in rural areas where traditional culture is still sufficiently rooted, myths, legends, folktales, riddles, and proverbs are still an important aspect of social life. Even for modern-day writers, traditional forms of oral literature have been inspirational. Pepetela's novel *Lueji* is based on Lunda's oral traditions. Many other writers such as Raúl David, José Luandino Vieira, Joaquim Cordeiro da Matta, Óscar Ribas, and António Jacinto have borrowed freely from the rich reserve of Angolan oral traditions, indigenous languages, and elements of African culture to place an African stamp on Angolan literature. Some scholars have made efforts to collect and preserve in writing the oral traditions of many Angolan languages.[10] An example is Raúl David, who has worked with Umbundu language and whose works include *Cantares do nosso Povo* (*Songs of Our People,* 1987), poems and songs in the Umbundu language.

Contemporary literature combines a variety of political, economic, and social themes and has addressed wide-ranging issues such as political corruption, the continued violence in the country, and urban poverty. Contemporary literature is dominated by established and well-known writers such as Pepetela, Manuel Rui, Henrique Abranches and Arnaldo Santos. Emerging writers, including José Eduardo Agualusa, José Sousa Jamba, Boaventura Cardoso, Fernando Fonseca Santos, Cikakata Mbalundo, Fragata de Morais, Jacinto de Lemos, Roderick Nehone, Alberto Oliveira Pinto, and Jacques Arlindo dos Santos, also have begun to make their mark. This generation of Angolan writers began to move away from the preoccupation with historical and political themes. Enjoying a greater freedom of literary creativity, they explore a new diversity of themes, ranging from romance to detective fiction. Pepetela's latest works are the detective novels *Jaime Bunda, Agente Secreto* (*Jaime Bunda, Secret Agent,* 2001) and *Jaime Bunda e a Morte do Americano* (*Jaime Bunda and the Death of an American,* 2003).

Also, Angolan writers have tended to broaden the geographic settings of their works. In the past, it was common for writers to set their novels in urban areas, particularly Luanda, which for ages was the center of social, political, and economic power in Angola. José Agualusa's *A Conjura* (*The Conspiracy,* 1989) is a typical novel based in Luanda. More recent works, however, have been set in Benguela and smaller towns, even in rural areas and in interior and southern regions.

A number of important developments have advanced the course of Angolan literature. The annual National Day of Culture showcases and celebrates the country's literature. This cultural event, held on January 8 every year, is a tribute to the legacy of Agostinho Neto, the poet-president who contributed significantly to Angolan culture in general and who helped place its literature on the literary map.

Literary organizations in Angola have contributed their share as well to the development of literature. The Union of Angolan Writers (União dos Escritores Angolanos, UEA), with headquarters at Luanda, was established after independence by a number of leading writers such as Vieira, who served for a while as its general secretary, and others like Pepetela and Rui. The UEA has hosted many literary events, instituted literary prizes, and contributed immensely to the publishing industry by publishing the works of many writers. For instance, Ana Tavares's *Ritos de passagem* (*Rites of Passage,* 1985) and Amelia da Lomba's *Noites ditas à chuva* (*Nights' Speeches to Rain,* 2005), both books of poetry, were published by the UEA. Established writers such as Henrique Abranches and Manuel Rui Monteiro have also been published by the UEA.

Other literary organizations include the Union of Angolan Artists and Composers, the Society of Angolan Authors, the Angolan Association of Theater, and the Angolan Youth Literature Brigade (BJLA). The BJLA in particular has been instrumental in the development of children's literature and has contributed to the enhancement of the culture of reading among the youth. It has sponsored lectures, seminars, workshops, school programs, and book fairs on children's literature. It has also promoted the works of Angolan writers of children's literature. One of the most popular works of children's literature is *O círculo de giz de bombó* (*The Manioc Chalk Circle,* 1979), a play by Henrique Guerra.

The award of honors recognizing the works of writers has also contributed to the development of literature. Angolan writers have benefited from both international and national honors. One of the first prestigious international awards to an Angolan writer was bestowed on Vieira in 1965 when *Luuanda* won the Grande Prémio de Novelística da Sociedade Portuguesa de Escritores (Grand Prize for Fiction of the Society of Portuguese Writers) in Lisbon. This award was instrumental in the internationalization of Angolan literature. In 1977, Pepetela won the prestigious international Camões Prize (Prémio Camões), which is the preeminent literary award for Lusophone literature jointly awarded annually by Portugal's Fundação Biblioteca Nacional (National Library Foundation) and Brazil's Departamento Nacional do Livro (National Book Department). This award is given to a work of Lusophone literature of distinction.

Another international literary award is Prémios da SONANGOL (SONANGOL Prize for Literature), awarded by the national oil company of Angola, SONANGOL. The award, which includes a cash prize of $50,000 (initially $25,000) for unpublished books, is designed to enhance the work of writers in Lusophone Africa. Originally, the award was given to writers in Angola, Cape Verde, and São Tomé and Príncipe but was broadened in 2004 to make Mozambican writers eligible. Angolan writer Jacques Arlindo dos Santos and poet Adriano Botelho de Vasconcelos have won the award.

A number of important national and local awards are presented as well. One is the National Prize for Literature (Premio Nacional de Literatura), which has been bestowed on notable writers such as Pepetela for his novel *Mayombe*. Another award is the Alda Lara Prize (Prémio Alda Lara), instituted in honor of the versatile female poet Alda Ferreira Pires Barreto de Lara Albuquerque, who died in January 1962. A set of prose and poetry prizes, each worth $35,000, was established by the UEA and the Ministry of Culture in 2004. SONANGOL also established a prize, the Revelation Prize, in 1999 exclusively for unpublished Angolan writers to encourage young writers and promote creative writing.

Since the end of the civil war, Angolan writers have been honored in other ways. In February 2005, the Benguela government announced it would name a street after deceased writer Raúl David.[11] David, who was born in Ganda, Benguela Province, in 1918, has made a significant contribution to Angola's literary tradition, especially its oral literature. Another form of honor is the issuance of special stamps for two distinguished and well-deserved writers, Agostinho Neto and Antonio Jacinto.

Fiction

Modern Angolan fiction has been dominated by the dual themes of the anticolonial nationalist struggle and the failure of a viable postindependence Angolan state. A great number of the modern writers emerged during the nationalist movement period, and many have continued to write to the present day. Some of the most distinguished writers are novelists such as Pepetela, Vieira, Rui, and Xitu.

Perhaps, the most celebrated Angolan writer today is the playwright and novelist Pepetela. Born in Benguela in 1941, he was a veteran of the anticolonial struggle, which reflected greatly in his literature. He is an internationally known writer who has produced more than a dozen major works of fiction, which include a novella, *As aventuras de Ngunga* (*Adventures of Ngunga*, 1972), and novels such as *Mayombe* (1980), *Yaka* (1984), *O Cão e os Caluandas* (*The Dog and the People of Luanda,*1985), *Lueji* (1991), *A geração da utopia* (*The Utopian Generations,* 1992), and *O Desejo de Kianda* (*The Return of the Water Spirit,* 1995).[12]

Another versatile Angolan writer is Luandino Vieira, who is noted for short stories and novels. He was born in Portugal in 1935, and although he was of Portuguese parentage, he had spent his youth in the *musseques* of Luanda when his parents immigrated to Angola in 1938. Vieira's familiarity with life in Luanda's poor neighborhoods greatly influenced his literature. For instance, his language of expression, as seen in his collection of short stories, *Luuanda,* combines Portuguese and Kimbundu, a blend of languages typical of the *musseques.* Much of his work, like those of other writers of his generation, portrays the harsh life of most Angolans during Portuguese colonialism. The publication of *Luuanda* in 1964 won him accolades and respectability in and outside Angola for the expression, in a vivid and candid manner, of the realities of the oppressed Angolan in the slums of Luanda. His other important works a novella, *A Vida Verdadeira de Domingos Xavier* (*The Real Life of Domingos Xavier,* 1974), *Velhas Estórias* (*Old Stories,* 1974), *Nós os do Makulusu* (*We, Those from Makulusu,* 1974), *Vidas Novas* (*New Lives,* 1975), and *João Vêncio: os sues Amores* (*João Vêncio: Regarding His Loves,* 1979).[13]

Manuel Rui is another leading Angolan fiction writer. He was born in 1941 in Nova Lisboa (now Huambo) and was very much active in the cultural and political life of his country after its independence. His large literary output included works like *Regresso Adiado* (*Delayed Return,* 1973), *Cinco Dias depois da Independencia* (*Five Days after Independence,* 1979), *Quem Me Dera Ser Onda* (*I Would Like to Be a Wave,* 1980), *Crónica de um Mujimbo* (*Mujimbo Chronicles,* 1989), *O Morto e os Vivos* (*The Dead and the Living,* 1993), *Rioseco* (*Dry River,* 1997), *Da Palma da Mão* (*From the Palm of the Hand,* 1998), *Saxofone e Metáfora* (*Saxophone and Metaphor,* 2001), and *Um Anel na Areia* (*A Ring in the Sand,* 2002).[14]

The writer Agostinho André Mendes de Carvalho, whose Kimbundu pen name is Uanhenga Xitu, is another important fiction writer in Angola whose prose best exemplifies the linguistic experiment characteristic of modern

Angolan narrative fiction. Xitu is noted for the use of a mixture of Kimbundu and Portuguese, which makes his works an expression of the colonial period cultural assimilation. His works include *Manana* (1974), *"Mestre" Tamoda e Outros Contos* (*"Master" Tamoda and Other Stories,*1977), *Maka na Sanzala* (*Maka in Sanzala,* 1979), *Os Sobreviventes da Máquina Colonial Depõem* (*The Survivors from the Colonial Machine Testify,* 1980), and *Os Discursos do "Mestre" Tamoda* (*The World of "Master" Tamoda,* 1984).[15]

Poetry

Although poetry was mainly unwritten in much of the precolonial period, it was nevertheless an integral part of the literatures of Angola. Poetry existed in the form of proverbs, riddles, and songs and was offered in indigenous languages. The development of modern poetry, however, could be partly attributed to a number of literary journals produced during the 1940s through the 1960s that helped build a generation of modern writers. First was a Portuguese journal, *Cultural,* which was published between 1945 and 1951, to which writers like Agostinho Neto contributed. In 1948, a group of Angolan intellectuals formed the Movement of Young Angolan Intellectuals and in 1950 published the *Antologia dos novos poetas de Angola (Anthology of New Poets of Angola),* in which they expressed their views. This publication was followed by the literary review *Mensagem (Message),* based in Luanda. For poets such as Agostinho Neto, António Jacinto, Alda Lara, and Mario Pinto de Andrade, the review provided an avenue of literary expression.[16] *Mensagem* was published for only two years, from 1951 to 1952, and only four issues saw publication before it was suppressed by the Salazar dictatorship. Succeeding *Mensagem* was another publication, *Cultura,* reissued in Luanda between 1957 and 1961 and sponsored by the Angolan Cultural Society (Sociedade Cultural de Angola). *Cultura* was more elaborate in its literary coverage than the previous publications, and it served to establish new poets. It became an outlet of poetic expression for writers such as Luandino Vieira, António Cardoso, and Henrique Abranches. Between 1953 and 1965, another literary publication, *Jornal de Angola,* was published to which many up-and-coming writers contributed.[17]

Although poetry was mainly cultural in theme and embedded in folk tradition during the precolonial period, it assumed a more political form in the colonial era. It served to critique the colonial system as evident in the works of many poets such as Mário Andrade, a foundation member of the MPLA and its president until 1962. Andrade was one of the early prominent Angolan poets whose works such as *Antologia da poesia negra de expressão portuguesa (Anthology of Black Poetry in Portuguese),* published in 1958, opposed Portuguese colonial rule.

During the anticolonial struggle, political poetry applauded the nationalist movement and sought to legitimize the demand for independence. Active in the liberation movement, like Andrade, was Agostinho Neto, who also was to head the MPLA and eventually become Angola's first president. Neto's poetry is perhaps the best example of revolutionary Angolan poetry. In 1974, the former president, the most notable of the Angolan poets, published *Sagrada Esperança (Sacred Hope),* a collection of poems about the anticolonial struggle.[18] Other notable poets are José Luis Mendonca, João Maimona, João Joao Melo, Lopito Feijoo, and Botelho de Vasconcelos.

Since independence an increased expression of poetry activities has occurred. New poets such as Ana Paula Tavares have joined long-established ones to promote the fortunes of poetry. The avenues of presentation of creative talents have increased through reading opportunities and slightly through publication. It must be noted, however, that access to published literary works generally and poetry in particular in Angola is still rather difficult. A great many poetry works are thus self-published.

Drama

Drama is the least developed literary form in Angola. The genesis of dramatic literature may be traced to the performance of a bilingual musical, *Bride Price,* in Luanda in 1971. Early written plays before independence included Armando Correia de Azevedo's *A Taberna (The Tavern)* and *Mull (Reflection)* and Domingos Van-Dunem's self-published *Auto de Natal (Christmas Play,* 1972). During the war of independence, a number of revolutionary performances were promoted by the nationalist leaders to boost the liberation struggle. Although not many plays have been published by writers, drama has made some appreciable development with the increasing establishment of urban theater groups. Stage shows and radio dramas also have become more popular. An example of a contemporary radio drama is *Camatondo,* a serial on postwar reconciliation efforts in Angola jointly produced by Rádio Nacional de Angola and the United Nations Integrated Regional Information Networks (IRIN) of Southern Africa.

Angola has a few prominent modern writers of drama. One of the most enterprising playwrights is José Mena Abrantes, who has written a number of plays such as *Ana, Zé e os Escravos (Ana, Zé and the Slaves,* 1988), *Nandyala ou a Tirania dos Monstros (Nandyala, or the Tyranny of Monsters,* 1993), *Sequeira, Luís Lopes ou o mulato dos prodígios (Luis Lopes Sequeira or the Mullato of the Prodigies,* 1993), and *A órfã do rei (The King's Orphan,* 1996). Apart from producing some of these plays for the theater, he has directed those of other writers. Although better known for his fiction, Pepetela is another writer who has written important plays. His one-act play *A Corda (The Rope),* published in 1978, is credited as the first full-fledged play, although it is not of particularly important literary interest.[19] In 1979, Pepetela published a second play, *A Revolta da Casa dos Ídolos* (The Revolt of the House of Idols), which was more successful than the first. Manuel Rui has also written and directed plays, among which are *O Espantalho* (*The Scarecrow,* 1973) and *Meninos de Huambo* (*Children of Huambo,* 1985). Other drama works have been produced, such as *O Círculo de Giz de Bombó* (*The Bombo Chalk-Circle,* 1979), a children's play by Henrique Guerra; *No Velho Ninguém Toca* (*No One Touches the Old Man,* 1979) by Fernando Costa Andrade; *O Panfleto* (*The Pamphlet,* 1988) by Domingos Van-Dunem; and *Diálogo com a Peripécia* (*Dialogue with Incidents,* 1987) by João Maimona.

A number of theater groups are active in Angola. A group, Horizonte Njinga Mbandi, was founded in Luanda in 1986 and has already performed many theater productions in Angola and even in other countries such as Portugal and Burkina Faso. In July 2005, Horizonte produced a play in Luanda, *O prato do cão* (*Dog's Meal*), that explores the theme of injustices in the workplace. Other theater groups such as Tchinganje, Xilenga, and Elinga Teatro were founded by Abrantes.

WOMEN WRITERS

Angolan women have played an important role in the literary development of the country.[20] A prominent early writer was Alda Ferreira Pires Barreto de Lara Albuquerque, who was born in Benguela in 1930. She was poet with a considerable literary output, but her main works were not published until after her death in January1962. After her death, a literary prize, the Alda Lara Prize (Prémio Alda Lara) was instituted in her honor. Published posthumously were her works *Poemas* (*Poems,* 1966), *Tempo da Chuva* (*Time of Rain,* 1973), *Poesia* (*Poetry,* 1979), and *Poemas* (*Collected Poems,* 1984). Other early published writers included Maria Archer, author of short fiction, legends, proverbs, and *Africa Selvagem: Folclore dos Negros do Grupo 'Bantu'* (a book of Bantu folklore, 1935); Emilia de Sousa Costa, a children's fiction writer and author of *Joanito Africanista* (*Joanito, the Africanist,* 1949); and Lília da Fonseca, novelist and poet, author of a number of books, including *Panguila* (1944), *Poemas da hora presente* (*Poems of the Present,* 1958), *Filha de Branco, Coleção Imbondeiro* (*The White's Daughter,* 1960), and *O relógio parado* (1961). Many of the early writers such as Maria da Luz Monteiro Macedo, Maria do Carmo Marcelino, Linda Martins, and Sofia da Costa Moura were self-published. For women writers, even the well-established ones, publication of their works remains a challenging task.

Nevertheless, women writers have published literature in prose, verse, and drama. One of the most prominent contemporary poets is Ana Paula Tavares, who was born in Lubango, in Huíla Province, in 1952. Tavares is a widely published feminist poet whose poetry has appeared in *Poesie d'Afrique au Sud du Sahara, 1945–1995 (African Poetry South of the Sahara, 1945–1995)* (1996), a UNESCO publication. Often sensual in tone, her works focus on postindependence Angola, especially the condition of women. She also has explored nature and stories of animals. Her books of poetry include *Ritos de Passagem (Rites of Passage, 1985), O Lago da Lua (The Lake of the Moon,* 1999), and *Dizes-me coisas amargas como os frutos (Tell Me of Bitter Things like Fruit,* 2001). She has also written prose works such as *O sangue da buganvilia (The Blood of the Bougainvillea,* 1997).

Angola has younger female writers as well, such as the poets Maria Alexandre Daskalos and Ana de Santana. Daskalos was born in 1957, and her works, in one essence, express deep sensitivity to nature and beauty and, in another, a dream, if forlorn, of perfection in a devastated society. One of her most important works is *Jardim das Delicias (Garden of Delights),* published in 1991. Santana, born in 1960, has written romantic poems, as seen in her book of poetry *Sabores, Odores & Sonho (Flavors, Scents and Reveries,* 1985).

Children's literature has been particularly popular with women writers. Active in this genre are writers like Maria Neto, Cremilde de Lima, Rosalina Pombal, Maria Celestina Fernandes, Maria da Conceição Figueiredo, and Maria de Jesus Haller. Neto, for instance, has turned out an impressive volume of work on children's literature, which includes *E na floresta os bichos falaram (The Animals Spoke in the Forest,* 1977), *A formação de uma estrela e outras histórias (The Rising of the Star and other Stories,* 1979), *As nossas mãos constroem a liberdade (Our Hands Are Forging Freedom,* 1979), *A lenda das asas e da menina Mestiça-Flor (The Legend of Wings and the Mulatta-Flower Girl,* 1981), *A menina Euflores Planeta da estrela Sikus (The Flower Planet Girl and the Sikus Star,* 1988), *A trepadeira ue queria ver of céu azul eoutras histórias (The Creeper Who Wanted to see the White Sky and Other Stories,* 1984), and *O vaticínio da Kianda na piroga do tempo (Kianda's Prophecy in the Canoe of Time,* 1989). New women writers have emerged in Angola, among which is Marta Medina, who recently published her first novel, *Escritório (Office,* 2005). Most of the new writers have self-published their works.

LITERATURE AND EXTERNAL INFLUENCE

The development of modern literature in Angola has benefited to some extent from external influences. First, in addition to Portuguese cultural influences, Angolan literature has been significantly impacted by black African literary traditions, notably Negritude. Although Negritude literature mainly expresses itself in French, it does help define Angola's national literature. For many Angolan writers, including Agostinho Neto, Negritude poetry directly inspires their works and serves as a literary model. Neto and other writers such as Vieira were also influenced by Brazilian literature.

An important contribution to the development of Angola's literature was also provided by Cuban literature. The Cubans claim historical affinity with the Angolans as a result of the Atlantic slave trade that transported thousands of Africans from the Angolan coast to the Caribbean. After the Angolan war of independence in 1975, Cuba sent its forces to Angola to provide military assistance to the MPLA government against South Africa's efforts to destabilize the newly independent state. Cuba also provided economic assistance to Angola through Cuban doctors, teachers, and engineers sent to the country. Cuban forces, about 50,000, and other personnel were finally withdrawn from Angola in 1991.

The presence of Cubans in Angola generated an entire literature, prose and verse, on the Angolan situation. Upon their return to Cuba, those who were inclined to write, especially combatants, put to paper their experiences in Angola. Don Burness has observed a number of facts about Cuban literature on Angola. First, he claims that many of those who wrote about Angola were already established writers and that the vast majority of them were white, or mulattoes, rather than Afro-Cubans, as one would have expected. Second, according to Burness, Cuban writers expressed different perceptions of Angola in their writings. The works of poets such as Joel James and Waldo Leyva show deep affection for Angola. Poets such as Antonio Conte and Victor Casaus express less affection. The works of writers such as short-story writer Rafael Carallero and poet Benito Estrada Fernández do not portray a favorable impression of Angola.[21]

A spirit of camaraderie, however, did exist between many Angolan and Cuban writers. The writers union in Angola encouraged this spirit of friendship by welcoming Cuban writers into the Angolan literary circles. Leading writers from the two nations maintained contacts. A number of Cuban authors were published in Angola journals, anthologies, and other literary avenues. Cuban literature, particularly those about Angola, found an important audience in the African country.[22]

STYLE IN ANGOLAN LITERATURE

A number of stylistic elements are evident in Angolan fiction. One is powerful imagery and symbolism, often used judiciously by fiction writers. The rich display of imagery is portrayed, for example, in Pepetela's *Yaka*, in which the birth of his main character, Alexandre Semedo, at the beginning of the novel signifies the debilitating and disruptive effects of colonialism on Angola. Pepetela writes of Alexandre's first cry:

It had the effect of a gunshot. Monkeys leapt from crags and were lost in the branches of swollen baobabs. Birds of every hue availed themselves of it to vanish beyond the Serra da Chela mountain range. Bush goats, zebras, even leopards, all hid in the folds of the Serra. Lizards and snakes slithered their sinuous bodies into holes and behind rocks.

There remained in the air the echo of the wail and the fearful mantle of silence that followed the violation. Long after Alexandre had spoken his first word, things and beings still looked at one another and looked out, waiting.[23]

Also in *Yaka,* the author uses the Yaka statue both as a representation of the evil that Portuguese colonialism stood for and the inevitability of the triumph of a new and free Angola. Alexandre's grandson, Joel, vividly portrays the symbolism of the corruption of colonialism in his explanation of the Yaka status to his grandfather: "The status represents a settler, grandfather. Look at it. It's what the sculptor thought of the settlers. He ridiculed them. Look at the nose. Stupid and ambitious."[24]

When Alexandre offers Joel the dagger, it is a symbolic endorsement of the guerrilla war of independence. The Yaka statue then assumes the second symbolic meaning, the resilience of the African culture, culminating in the end of colonialism and the emergence of a new Angola.

Irony is also prevalent in contemporary Angolan narrative fiction, as evident in the works of many of the leading authors such as Pepetela, Manuel Rui, Manuel dos Santos Lima, and Uanhenga Xitu. They use irony to critique the sorry state of political and economic affairs in contemporary Angola as evident in Lima's novel *Os anões e os Mendigos* (*The Dwarves and the Beggars,* 1984), which is set in an imaginary nation, Silver Coast.

Through a blend of the Portuguese language with local languages, Angolan writers also have devised a unique language that has enabled them to fashion modern national literature congruent to the nation's culture. The so-called Angolanidade of the Portuguese language is reflected in the works of writers such as Boaventura Cardoso and Manuel Rui. Also, for many of the modern writers such as Xitu and Vieira, an important aspect of their works is the incorporation of elements of traditional literature such as myths, legends, folktales, and proverbs.

MAJOR ANGOLAN WRITERS OF THE TWENTIETH CENTURY

In terms of periodization, Angolan writers fall roughly into three groups. The first group consists of writers who were well known during the colonial period, roughly from the early twentieth century to the 1930s. They include Pedro da Paixão Franco, Augusto Tadeu Bastos, Óscar Ribas, and António de Assis Jr. The second group of writers became prominent during the anti-colonial movement and the immediate postindependence period. Some of the prominent ones in this group are Agostinho Neto, António Jacinto, Raúl David, Luandino Vieira, Henrique Abranches, Uanhenga Xitu, Manuel Rui, Pepetela, Jorge Macedo, Paula Tavares, José Mena Abrantes, and Boaventura Cardoso. The third group gained prominence in the 1980s, 1990s, and later. In this group are Carmo Neto, João Tala, José Eduardo Agualusa, Rui Augusto, Jacinto de Lemos, Lopito Feijoó, João Melo, and João Maimona.[25]

MASS MEDIA

From the colonial period, the Angolan press has lacked freedom of opinion and expression. Portuguese colonialism was repressive and intolerant of any form of opposition. The colonial authority thus stifled journalism and curtailed the expression of anticolonial sentiments. Journalists who criticized the colonial system were often subjected to persecution.

At independence, the ruling MPLA declared a Marxist state that by nature was intolerant of dissent. Under the MPLA dictatorship, the Angolan press continued under strict government and party control. Despite the guarantee of freedom of expression by the Angolan constitution, the MPLA government nationalized both the print and broadcast media, making press freedom virtually nonexistent. Government control of mass media and press censorship greatly discouraged critical editorials and publication of news items considered by the state as unfriendly. Only official state policy was permitted publication or broadcast. Journalists working with state-run media such as Rádio Nacional de Angola (National Radio of Angola, RNA), Televisão Pública de Angola (Public Television of Angola, TPA), and *Jornal de Angola* operated under direct control of the minister of mass media, who ensured that nothing critical of the government was published or broadcast. Even when independently run media came into existence, they had to contend with strict state censorship. The press, under state control, thus virtually became an appendage of the government. The Angolan professional journalists' body, the Uniao dos Jornalistas (the Journalists' Union, UAJ), was required to work hand in hand with the government and to follow established laws and regulations governing the practice of journalism. Describing state censorship of the press, journalist João Pokongo stated:

You have to remember that information is a monopoly of the party. Every year the MPLA draws up a directive to determine editorial policy. On top of that, there is day-to-day control. In any case, every journalist knows and has a duty to know the essential party line; he has to know this first so that his writings are in line with it.[26]

The civil war further led to the tightening of government control over the mass media. In 1999, the government imposed a news embargo on the war. The MLPA government required absolute loyalty of the press and forbade journalists from publishing anything critical of the state or the party. Opposition newspapers were banned, and journalists sympathetic to the rebel movement, National Union for the Total Independence of Angola (União Nacional para a Independência Total de Angola, UNITA), were persecuted. UNITA itself severely restricted press freedom in the areas it controlled.

In the intolerant atmosphere of the fratricidal civil war, journalists were constantly harassed. It became virtually impossible to disseminate news unfettered in such an environment. The ethnic, political, and ideological polarization that characterized the conflict did not give way to open and free expression of thought.

The Lusaka Protocol of 1994 between the government and UNITA proposed the use of mass media as instruments of national reconciliation. Consequently, the protocol provided for freedom of speech and of the press. In the late 1990s, various governmental officials, including President dos Santos, professed greater press freedom. In December 1995, the president reportedly described his country as the "New Mecca" of freedom of expression in Africa and affirmed that "we have a good relationship with the press."[27] In April 1996, at the inception of the government of national unity, the president declared a new direction in allowing press freedom.

The Angolan government did not live up to its profession of free expression. Mass media organizations critical of the government or perceived as threats to the establishment were always under the dangling sword of proscription. Journalists who expressed opinions contrary to official policy continued to be harassed. Some experienced detention or jail terms without trial, and others were relived of their positions. Even journalists have been reportedly murdered, presumably by government agents and apparently for critical reporting or for refusal to tow the official state line. According to a report by the Committee to Protect Journalists, between 1994 and 1998 five journalists were murdered in Angola, all of them known for their critical reporting about the government.[28]

The arrest in late 1999, detention, and subsequent conviction of prominent journalist and human rights activist Rafael Marques provide a good example of the oppressive atmosphere in which representatives of the media had to do their work. Marques, a columnist with the privately owned weekly *Folha 8* had published an article in the July 3, 1999, issue of the paper that was critical of President dos Santos. In the article, titled "The Lipstick of Dictatorship," Marques had biting words for the president to whom he referred as a "dictator." He accused the president of bearing the "responsibility for the destruction of the country" and of being "accountable for the promotion of incompetence, embezzlement and corruption."[29] For this article, Marques was charged with defamation and slander, convicted, and was fined and given a six-month suspended sentence. Subsequently, however, Marques continued to be harassed by the state.

NEWSPAPERS AND MAGAZINES

Although the press has not been free in Angola, the nation boasts scores of newspapers and magazines. In 1995, the minister of information, Pedro Hendrik Vaal Neto, reported that 40 newspapers, 24 magazines, and 18 bulletins existed in Angola.[30] Since the end of the civil war, many more publications have been established.

Newspapers and magazines in Angola can be divided into two categories. First are the government-owned and state-controlled publications such as *Jornal de Angola.* This paper published in Luanda in Portuguese is the only national daily. The government also publishes *Diário de República* and *Diário de Luanda.*

The second category comprises privately owned, independent papers. Leaders in this category are the weekly *Folha 8, Agora,* and *Comércio Actualidade.* Others include the Luanda-based biweekly *A capital* and the weekly *Angolense,* also based in Luanda. In addition are other papers such as the weekly *Actual, Tempos Novos, O Independente, Imparcial Fax,* and the Roman Catholic newspaper *Apostolado.* Some of these nonaligned papers have demonstrated their ability, at lest to some extent, to critique the government. For instance, on a number of occasions, to the chagrin of the government, *Folha 8* published a series on human rights in Angola. Attempts by these independent papers to be vocal have been met with state reprisals.

In addition to these two categories are papers with links to the major political organizations and parties. For example, Luanda-based weekly publications such as *Correio da Semana* and *Era Nova* are linked to the MPLA. *Terra Angolana,* an irregularly published paper that debuted with the ceasefire brought about by the Bicesse Accord, was linked to UNITA. Another UNITA opposition paper was *O Voz do Trabalhador,* a monthly newsletter that expressed views different from the government.

The Angolan print media have faced numerous problems. Primary is lack of adequate financial resources to stay afloat. Privately owned news media have suffered particularly from lack of adequate funds to publish regularly. Many of them could not enjoy support either from the state or from the business community that regarded them as antigovernment. Thus, their publications remained erratic. For instance, the private paper *Angolense* temporarily ceased publication in 2000 because of financial problems.

The second problem is one of distribution. Only the state press has the ability to distribute widely and even sometimes nationwide. The private press usually find it difficult to reach beyond major urban centers like Luanda and Benguela, primarily because they lack the financial resources to distribute and also because some provinces will not tolerate critical papers.

For the most part, journalism is not exactly a well-paid venture in Angola. In particular, journalists working in private newspapers are often not professionally trained and are underpaid. Not only are they poorly paid, they work in poor environments as well and lack adequate modern tools of the trade like computers.

RADIO AND TELEVISION

Angola has only one nationwide radio station, Rádio Nacional de Angola. Initially, the government forbade the operation of private or shortwave radio stations. By 2000, however, the country boasted 36 AM, 7 FM, 9 shortwave radio stations, and 7 television stations.[31] Since then, the number of radio stations has risen considerably. Broadcast is mainly in Portuguese, but some broadcasts are in indigenous languages.

Apart from the state-controlled Rádio Nacional, the largest of the radio stations in Angola, a number of privately owned independent stations exist. Most of the stations are based in Luanda. A major one is Luanda Antena Comercial (Luanda Commercial Radio, LAC). Other Luanda-based FM stations are Radio 5 (RNA), Radio FM Estereo (RNA), Radio Luanda (RNA), and Radio N'Gola Yetu (RNA).

FM and shortwave stations operate in other parts of Angola as well. FM stations include Radio Cabinda Comercial, which operates in Cabinda City; Radio Morena in Benguela; and Radio 2000 in Lubango. Shortwave stations are Emissora Províncial Kuando-Kubango in Menongue in Cuando-Cubango Province; Emissora Províncial da Huíla in Lubango, Huíla Province; Emissora Províncial do Namibe in Namibe, Namibe Province; and Emissora Províncial de Benguela in Benguela, Benguela Province.

Even though many of these stations could be classified as independent, they shy away from overtly criticizing the government. This is true of even major stations such as Luanda Antena Comercial, Radio Cabinda Comercial, Radio Morena, and Radio 2000. Established shortly before the 1992 elections through discreet financial backing of the MPLA, they served as an instrument of electioneering for the party.[32] A more independent station, however, is Radio Ecclesia, the Roman Catholic–owned radio that made its debut in December 1954 and began broadcasting 24 hours a day in 1969. This station has criticized the government on occasion, especially on its dismal human rights record. It has broadcast dissenting views and breached the official ban placed on reporting the civil war. In 1977, the government expropriated the station but returned it to the church in 1979.

During the late 1980s, UNITA operated a propaganda radio station, A Voz da Resistência do Galo Negro (Voice of the Resistance of the Black Cockerel, VORGAN). Broadcasting in Portuguese and local languages, this station transmitted from installations inside apartheid South Africa to central and southern Angola. Its purpose was to serve UNITA's cause and to oppose the Luanda government.

Television service in Angola was initially available in Luanda and its environs in 1976. Angola's state-controlled television station is Televisão Pública de Angola (Public Televsion of Angola, TPA), which runs two channels.

NEWS AGENCIES

The sole and official news agency in Angola is ANGOP, a public enterprise established in Luanda in July 1975 that presumably enjoys autonomy and editorial independence under Angola's laws. Its main functions are to gather and process news items about Angola and the world in general and to distribute Angolan news to national and international media organizations.[33]

Through agreement, ANGOP has worked with foreign media organizations. Active in Angola are foreign press agencies such as the French Agence France-Presse and the Pan-African News Agency. Before the collapse of the Soviet Union, the Soviet news agency, TASS, was allied with ANGOP. Apart from the Soviet Union, other Eastern European countries and China maintained media offices in Angola. Also, the Cuban-based Latin American news agency, Prensa Latina, operated in Luanda. Despite the repressive journalistic environment, the Angolan press has generally demonstrated at least an appreciable level of professionalism. Their main professional body, the União de Jornalistas, set up in May 1982, has been an instrument through which media workers struggle to establish press autonomy and freedom to disseminate information without fear of government reprisal. Although state influence on the mass media will probably continue, the ascendancy of press freedom in the real sense may be on the horizon. Recently, the government made a move to democratize the mass media by approving a new press. Mass

Media Deputy Minister Manuel Miguel de Carvalho explained: "When we say that the content of the document is democratic, we are referring to the fact that there had been eliminated all the constraints that were placed on radio and TV stations, among other issues."[34]

A way in which professionalism is rewarded is through awards to deserving journalists. One such award is the Maboque Journalism Award established in 1994 by a business management company, Maboque. The award, which carries a prize of about $35,000, is an annual recognition of a journalist who has produced the best news article. In 2005, the award was upgraded to make news agency staff and photojournalists eligible apart from professional journalists. Past winners of the award included Bie Radio journalists Faria Horacio and Abel Abraao; Mateus Goncalves, Alves Fernandes, Reginaldo Silva and Alves Antonio, Luisa Francony, Paulo Araujo, and Ismael Mateus, all of Luanda Antena Comercial; Luis Domingos and Isidro Sanhanga, both of Televisao Popular de Angola; and Benguela Radio journalist Jaime Azulay.

INTERNET

The Internet is rapidly becoming an important part of the Angolan communication culture. Apart from government departments and business enterprises, newspapers and broadcast stations have gone online. A number of news publications now provide electronic versions of their papers on the Internet. For instance, *Jornal de Angola* has an online version that features news about Angolan politics, culture, economics, sports, and general opinion.[35] The Angolan news agency, Agência Angola Press (ANGOP), also has a Web site that features Angolan politics, economy, society, sports, and culture and African and international news in three languages: Portuguese, English, and French.[36]

Other sources of current information about Angola exist on the Internet. The Angolan embassy in Washington, DC, has an electronic version of a bimonthly newsletter, *O Pensador*.[37] Angola's Permanent Mission to the United Nations also publishes a bimonthly Internet newsletter, *The Angolan Mission Observer*.[38] Other Angolan embassies in major Western capitals have informative Web sites.

A few radio stations have begun to broadcast on the Internet. These include Luanda Antena Comercial;[39] the Catholic station, Radio Ecclesia;[40] and Rádio Nacional.[41]

Internet access for the vast majority of Angolans is still, however, very much limited. In 2001, there were 30,000 Internet users, and only one Internet service provider existed in 2000.[42]

NOTES

1. Republic of Angola, *Newsletter of the Embassy of Angola in the UK.*
2. "Deputy Mass Media Minister on New Press Law."
3. An example is Pepetela's novel, *Yaka.*
4. See Chatelain, "King Kitamba Kia Xiba," in *Folk-Tales of Angola,* 223–27.
5. See Chatelain, "The Son of Kimanaueze and the Daughter of Sun and Moon," in *Folk-Tales of Angola,* 131–41.
6. Sanders, *A Collection of Umbundu Proverbs,* cited in http://www.afriprov.org/resources/dailyproverbs.htm.
7. Hamilton, *Voices from an Empire,* 34.
8. For a discourse on Soromenho, see ibid., 34–40.
9. Quoted in Leite, "Angola," 126.
10. Such an effort has been made, for instance, by the Departamento Nacional de Folklore, Secretaria de Estado da Cultura.
11. See Permanent Mission of the Republic of Angola to the United Nations, Newsletter no. 11.
12. For important discourses on Pepetela, see Peres, *Transculturation and Resistance,* chap. 4; and Clive Willis, "Pepetela," in Cox, African *Writers,* 685–95.
13. For discourses on Vieira, see Burness, *Fire,* 1–18; Peres, *Transculturation and Resistance,* chap. 2; and Phyllis Reisman Butler, "Writing a National Literature: The Case of José Luandino Vieira," in Reis, *Toward Socio-Criticism,* 135–42.
14. More detailed analysis of Manuel Rui is provided in Afolabi, *Golden Cage,* 77–116; and Peres, *Transculturation and Resistance,* chap. 5.
15. For a good analysis of Xitu and his work, see Peres, *Transculturation and Resistance,* chap. 3.
16. For a brief discussion of *Mensagem,* see Leite, "Angola," 143.
17. For general discussion of this subject, see Alao, "The Development of Lusophone African Literary Magazines," 169–83.
18. Agostinho Neto, *Sagrada Esperança* (Luanda: União dos Escritores Angolanos, 1979). The English translation of the book is Marga Holness, *Sacred Hope: Poems by Agostinho Neto* (Luanda: União, ENDIAMA, 1989). For more on Neto and his works, see Burness, *Fire: Six Writers from Angola,* 19–34.
19. See Leite, "Angola," 141.
20. For a comprehensive list of Lusophone women writers, see Gomes and Cavacas, *Dicionàrio de Autores de Literaturas de Língua Portuguesa.* Women writers from Angola are well represented in Simoes da Silva, *A Bibliography of Lusophone Women Writers.*
21. Burness, *On the Shoulder of Marti,* 4–5.
22. Ibid., 52–53.
23. Pepetela, *Yaka,* 3.
24. Ibid., 296.
25. See the detailed classification in Kandjimbo, "Verbetes: de escretories Angolanos."

26. Cited in Guimarães, "The Evils of Muzzled Press in Angola," 4.

27. Ibid., 3.

28. See Committee to Protect Journalists, "Country Report: Angola." See also Human Rights Watch, *Angola Unravels,* 81.

29. Marques, "The Lipstick of Dictatorship."

30. Human Rights Watch, *Angola Unravels,* 80.

31. Infoplease, "Angola."

32. Human Rights Watch, *Angola Unravels,* 83.

33. See ANGOP's Web site at http://www.angolapress-angop.ao/angop-e.asp.

34. "Deputy Mass Media Minister on New Press Law."

35. See *Jornal de Angola's* Web site at http://www.jornaldeangola.com/.

36. See ANGOP's Web site at http://www.angolapress-angop.ao/.

37. See *O Pensador's* Web site at http://www.angola.org/news/pensador/index.html.

38. See *The Angolan Mission Observer's* Web site at http://www.angola.org/news/mission/index.html.

39. See Luanda Antena Comercial's Web site at http://www.ebonet.net/lac.

40. See Radio Ecclesia's Web site at http://ecclesia.snet.co.ao.

41. See Rádio Nacional's Web site at http://www.rna.ao/.

42. Infoplease, "Angola."

4

Art, Architecture, and Housing

> Virtually every village had at least one practicing artist of more than routine skill, and most had several in different media, while every home had at least one object of merit.
> —Daniel J. Crowley, on Chokwe art[1]

ALTHOUGH ANGOLA HAS gone through many years of wars that caused untold destruction to the cultural infrastructure, the nation's rich artistic heritage has continued to flourish. Art in Angola is expressed in a wide range of media, including plastic, ceramic, wood, ivory, and metal. Different ethnic groups exhibit particular artistic styles. For instance, the Chokwe of northeastern Angola are highly skilled carvers who have produced some of the best sculptures in the country. Indeed, most Chokwe are able to make art objects, with men specializing in carving masks and statues and women usually producing a variety of handicrafts. Generally, popular forms of art in Angola include mask and sculpture carving, pottery making, textile designing, painting, beadwork, and body adornment.

The traditional art of Angola has a historical link with the culture of the people. Art did not exist merely for aesthetic value. Art was sacred; beyond visual appreciation, it was an integral part of ritual performances and other traditional ceremonies and festivals. In modern Angola, however, the cultural utility of art has greatly diminished. Art has increasingly been commercialized and has become the object of museum and gallery exhibits. The merchandizing of art derives from a new emphasis placed on its aesthetic value.

Angolan artistic expression is also seen in its architectural forms. Cities feature a blend of modern and colonial-style architecture. Public buildings are of modern Western-style and sometimes can be imposing, adding aesthetic

Angola is rich in different art forms particularly sculpturing and carving. Generally, art is for sale, obtainable in general and art markets as well as galleries. Courtesy of Armando J. Rodriguez, Jr.

quality to the city. In major urban centers such as Luanda, which developed as a center of colonial culture, Portuguese-style colonial architecture is evident. Many private homes, particularly in well-to-do districts, are modern, concrete-block, zinc-roofed buildings. In contrast to cities, mud architecture is common in rural settings. Many houses in the villages are of simple design, made out of mud bricks and roofed with thatch.

TRADITIONAL ART

Traditional art in Angola dates to the centuries of the development of the cultures of the peoples of Angola. The art of the Chokwe and related peoples is some of the best known in the world and predates the arrival of the Europeans in Angola. Marie-Louise Bastin, the Belgian art historian and authority on Chokwe art, has cited the existence of "a finely-sculptured zoomorphic wooden sculpture" as evidence of the antiquity of Chokwe art. According to Bastin, the wooden piece was more than a thousand years old and "is the oldest known wooden sculpture from central Africa."[2]

A great deal of what is regarded today as art was, in precolonial times, elements of ritual practices and cultural activities such as birth, puberty, circumcision, initiation, chieftaincy investiture, funeral rites, and other traditional ceremonies and festivals. Although traditional art is expressed in one form of ritual performance or the other, different regions or ethnolinguistic groups have unique artistic abilities. A history of intergroup interactions, however, has led to shared artistic values.[3]

Mask and Sculpture

Mask carving represents one of the most popular forms of traditional art in Angola. Masks are often carved out of wood, bronze, and other metals, and they usually represent the spirit of lineage, clan, or family ancestors; deities; mythological figures; and even animals. The most common masks are those used in initiation ceremonies such as healing, circumcision, fertility, and puberty rites. Also common are masks depicting the spirits of deities and ancestors. Ancestral worship is important in Angolan culture, and ancestral masks are used in ritual ceremonies in honor of deities.

Masks are not intended to be decorative; they are believed to possess great magical powers and, therefore, must be worn by designated people, often men, after the proper initiation or induction rite has been performed. The wearer of a spirit mask is believed to be in communion with the spirit world of deities and departed ancestors represented by the mask.

Masks in Angola are of various types and come in different shapes, sizes, and artistic quality. Some of the best known are produced by the Chokwe, such as the mask of their female ancestor Mwana Pwo (young maiden). A popular mask in Angola, it is used in puberty and fertility rituals. It is traditionally worn by male dancers dressed like women and sporting false breasts. The wooden mask has a facial appearance akin to a deceased person. Its facial scarification is a symbol of the pain of death, as Mwana Pwo was said to have died young. The mask is also adorned with beads, forehead cruciforms, woven headpieces, and other ornaments. Although the Chokwe ritual is performed by men, its mask is regarded as an embodiment of feminine beauty, which supposedly bestows fertility on women and prosperity on the people in general.

The male companion of Mwana Pwo is the mask of Cihongo (spirit of wealth). Its existence suggests that some masks are made in pairs or even in groups. The Cihongo mask is different from its female Pwo counterpart. Rather than a gaunt expression characteristic of the Pwo mask, Cihongo sports a fierce expression with wide mouth, elaborately painted white teeth, and exaggerated horizontal beard. The mask, which is carved from wood and worn exclusively by a designated chief or his sons, represents age, wealth, and chiefly power and authority.

Other ethnic groups in Angola have been greatly influenced by Chokwe art. Groups such as the Yaka, Mbunda, Lovale, Lunda, and others have produced impressive masks as well. The Yaka, for instance, have a variety of *mukanda* (initiation) masks, one of the most noted being the *ndemba*, which is used during initiation ceremonies for boys. This mask is a representation of the Yaka ancestor credited with establishing the initiation rite for young people. When adorned by the youngsters during the initiation ritual dance, the Yaka mask is believed to confer on the new initiates the regenerative quality of the ancestors. Different kinds of *ndemba* masks exist, but they are commonly wooden in texture with the face decorated with white paint. Among the Mbunda, the *makishi,* a mask worn by masqueraders during circumcision rites, is popular.

Many of the masks carved in Angola are worn with elaborate and complex body costumes made of cloth and plant fibers. The costumes are colorful and lavishly decorated with various objects such as beads. Some of the masks are adorned with braided hair intricately woven into them.

Apart from masks representing the human face, many Angolan masks depict various animals. Animal masks are quite popular because animals often feature in the mythology of many Angolan groups. Antelope, buffalo, elephant, zebra, monkey, leopard, rhino, pig, baboon, snake, and lizard masks are common. These masks, carved primarily in wood and sometimes in metal, are beautiful pieces of art. In traditional societies, however, animal masks primarily served as ritual objects in different kinds of ceremonies, such as initiation rites.

Sculpture is also a popular traditional art form in Angola noted among many ethnic groups such as the Chokwe, the Ovimbundu, the Imbangala, the Lwena, and the Luvala. Examples of Angolan sculpture are statues of royal figures such as kings, queens, and nobles; powerful warriors, hunters, and healers; musicians and ceremonial dancers; ancestors and deities; and mythical beings. Human statues are of varying size, from the tiny to life-size. They also are made in different postures; some are in standing position and others in sitting or kneeling position. Postures are not merely aesthetic, however; they have symbolic meaning. Statues are usually carved in solid wood and sometimes adorned with decorative metal.

In addition to human statues, carvings of court items and paraphernalia depict the glory, dignity, and pomp of royalty. Such royal carvings include chairs, stools, decorated thrones, ceremonial staffs, spears, and scepters. Other carvings are related to household objects such as chairs, tables, and stools and those of personal effects such as canes, combs, bracelets, necklaces, and headgear. Some carvings are of spiritual value, such as traditional worship figures found in shrines and other objects used in ritual performances.

The Chokwe are particularly adept sculptors who have produced some of the most famous sculptures and carvings of objects of everyday use.

Monuments dot the landscape of Angolan cities. The one
in this picture is a memorial to women who fought in the
independence war. Courtesy of Armando J. Rodriguez, Jr.

In traditional precolonial societies, sculpture was the exclusive preserve of
professional carvers known as the *songi,* who often worked exclusively for
the court and other prominent chieftaincies. They are noted for a variety of
masterpiece sculptures, including deified ancestors, elaborate statues of folk
figures, and objects of royalty such as thrones, stools, chairs, and headrests.
Demonstrating the Chokwe artistic finesse are a variety of impressively decorated ceremonial wooden stools. Some, for example, are carved with legs that
show male and female figures, whereas others show images of mother and
child.

The most widely known Angolan sculpture is the Chokwe statue the
"Thinker" ("Pensador" in Portuguese). One of the oldest artifacts in Angola,
it has become a symbol of national culture and is greatly revered. The statue
is represented as a man or a woman and depicts wisdom and knowledge. It
is carved in a bending position, hands on head and legs crossed, a posture
symbolizing reflection.[4]

One of the best known Angolan sculptures is the Chokwe statue, popularly known as Pensador, or the "thinker." A symbol of national culture, artists have produced many variations of the statue. Essentially, as seen in the picture above, it is depicted as a man or a woman, bent in a thinking mood with hands on head. Courtesy of Armando J. Rodriguez, Jr.

Also popular in Angola are the statues of the mythological royal Chokwe-Lunda couple, *chibinda* (hunter) Ilunga Ketele, and Princess Lweji. Ilunga, the Chokwe and Lunda civilizing cultural hero, is credited with the introduction of new hunting items such as bow, arrow, axe, and knife. He is therefore a symbol of hunting and is often represented by an impressive statue in which he is adorned in a hunting garb, brandishing a gun, and wearing a chief's hat. There are many other variations of this statue. Sometimes, he is depicted wearing an elaborate crown, a symbol of his royal status, and holding a staff and a horn containing hunting charms. The statue of Lweji complements that of Ilunga.[5] Lweji was the Lunda female chief, the mythical wife of Ilunga. Her statue is similar to that of Ilunga, except that it is a female figure, as evident by breasts and the wearing of headdress.

Among the Kongo, the unique sacred statues *minkisi* (singular, *nkisi*) or power figures represent fetishism. The statues are wooden figures, sometimes depicting humans or animals, and carry various fetish objects used to conjure spirit powers. The *nkisi* objects are of various types, including mirrors, gourd, and nails. These objects also serve various purposes and are used in divination, initiation, and other ceremonies.

Although masks and statues are primarily traditional, they are still part of Angola's modern-day art. Modern carvers continue to work in various media such as wood, ivory, and metal to produce traditional statues as decorative art. For the most part, masks and statues are no longer of major religious and traditional significance. Rather, they are increasingly commercialized and produced primarily as entertainment art with an eye for profit by anyone with the artistic know-how. Traditional art, particularly Chokwe sculpture, has been in great demand by art collectors around the world and is treasured in galleries, museums, and private collections. Angola's expatriate community and foreign visitors, especially Europeans, have been the major motivation for sculptors to produce. The "Thinker" is one of the most produced traditional decorative statues in Angola.

Metalwork

Another aspect of Angolan art is metalwork, popular among many ethnolinguistic groups. Traditional blacksmiths *(fuli)* specialize in working various objects—primarily weapons, tools, and decorations—from metal. These include various types of knives, daggers, hoes, spears, and swords. They are artistic in that they are not just made to serve their original purposes; they are also produced to show aesthetic quality. As technology is relatively underdeveloped in Angola, blacksmiths are still important at some levels.

Portuguese Influence on Traditional Art

Centuries of the Portuguese presence in Angola inevitably introduced Euro-Christian elements into the art of the people. Although traditional art was primarily embedded in African culture, as evident in the production of ritual masks as well as ancestral statues, sculptors have also carved various types of Christian religious icons. The most notable of these icons are metal statues of saints and crucifixes carved from brass or bronze.

Apart from carving overtly religious icons, Angolan sculptors incorporated into their traditional art Western values. For instance, the Chokwe and other groups eventually integrated Portuguese decorative motifs into traditional ceremonial chairs, stools, thrones, and other carvings.

MODERN ART

Modern art in Angola consists of different forms, the most important of which are painting, handicrafts, and textile and fashion designs. Unlike traditional art, modern art is produced solely for aesthetic value with a particular appeal to the tourist market. Modern art thus bears the imprint of so-called airport art, that is, commercial art that targets the foreign market, particularly European. These art forms are without regard to the cultural underpinnings that define traditional art.

Painting

As in most parts of southern Africa, the earliest form of painting in Angola is rock art. Painted figures such as those of animals have been discovered in a number of caves in Angola. Apart from rock painting, several Angolan ethnic groups such as the Chokwe and related peoples practiced an artistic tradition known as *sona* (sand drawing). Among the Chokwe, sand drawing consists of skillfully patterned lines drawn with geometric precision through a web of dots. The purpose of this form of ideogram is to illustrate folk stories, fables, proverbs, riddles, and jokes.[6]

In modern times, painting has become an important and popular art medium in Angola and is expressed in different forms such as watercolor, acrylic, pastel, and oil on canvas. Professional painters are some of the leading artists in Angola. Many have taken part in major exhibits in and outside Angola, and some have won important local and international awards.

Modern Angolan painting is defined by culture, tradition, historical experience, contemporary reality, and the physical environment. The civil war is a major theme of art and has produced powerful images of war's devastation. Also common in modern painting is portrait, particularly of heroic personalities. With many variations, Nzinga Mbande, the Ndongo and Matamba queen and an Angolan heroine, is perhaps the most painted historical figure.

A new generation of visual artists depict in their works a variety of images related to everyday life. Popular subjects for painters range from images of crime and poverty representing effects of urbanism to serene landscape representing the beauty of Angola. Increasingly, artists have also turned to wild display of colors and other forms of abstract expressionism.

Crafts

Handicrafts have always been an important part of Angolan art tradition. Pottery and basketry are among the more popular forms of handicrafts. These are created primarily by men, although many women are pottery makers. Pots are made primarily for household uses, for instance as water vessels and cooking utensils. They come in artistic styles, however, and are beautifully finished. Terra-cotta and ceramic pots may be colorfully decorated with items such as beads and hand-painted human and animal figures and sometimes geometrically aligned decorative patterns.

Basket making is popular as well in Angola. It is particularly the domain of women who make household baskets for family use, such as for the storage of grains, flour, and other food items. Baskets were also traditionally used in rituals such as divination because they held the objects required for such rituals. Craftsmen and women have continued to produce fine, hand-woven or plaited baskets in many different shapes. Basket design requires the weaver to be imaginative but meticulous to produce a fine and richly finished product. Baskets are usually made for sale or presented as gifts. Other forms of handicrafts are leatherwork, mat making, beadwork, and calabash engraving.

Textile Art

The weaving of cloth is an aspect of textile art and is historically well known in Angola. Cloth weaving is one of the art forms in which female creative expression is best demonstrated. In precolonial times, cloth was woven out of hand-spun cotton, but this weaving technique has declined with the advent of modern machine weaving.

Textile art in the form of making designs on cloth is still very popular. Angolan textile artists pay attention to rich displays of color, artistic patterns, and other decorative embellishments in their work. The most popular form of artistic design on textile is embroidery. During the colonial period, mission churches encouraged women to learn this skill, and in postconflict Angola, many Christian organizations and nongovernmental organizations working in-country have emphasized the same vocation for women. Embroidery is a technique through which complicated patterns are sewn on fabrics. Courtly regalia are some of the most elaborately embellished in this way and show royal prestige. Ceremonial dresses, especially for the well-to-do, are also often embroidered. Embroidering in the past was typically hand-sewn; however, machine embroidery has increasingly replaced hand embroidering. Embroidery is done on both men's and women's dress.

Another important artistic work on textile is the technique of cloth dyeing. Textile artists use different colors, but more often indigo, in coloring cloths. Various techniques are used in dyeing cloth. In some cases, the whole cloth is dyed; in other cases it is dyed using a specialized technique called tie-dyeing. The latter technique produces a more artistic pattern.

Artists

Angola boasts of a large assembly of artists representing every genre. Although many are not known beyond their immediate locale, quite a number are of national and international renown.

One of the most noted plastic artists of international stature was the painter Vitor Teixeira, who was born in Luanda in 1940 and died in 1993. Known simply as Viteix, this famous artist was educated in plastic arts in Angola, Portugal, and France. His art transcended various forms, including oils, engraving, and abstract painting. In addition to his native Angola, his works have been exhibited in many countries, including Portugal, France, Cuba, Brazil, and several other African countries. He was a winner of many awards in and outside of Angola.

Another highly accomplished artist is the multimedia artist António Ole, who was born in Luanda in 1951 of mixed origin. He is a sculptor, photographer, and film director. His art, most especially his painting, derives inspiration from authentic African culture as well as European influences. In other words, Ole has a global perspective on art in that he seeks to marry that which is Angolan with the foreign. He also uses traditional ritual icons to devise modern art that is relevant to contemporary reality. His work has won international recognition and has been exhibited across the globe. Other notable plastic artists include Augusto Ferreira de Andrade, Francisco Domingos Van-Dúnem, Jorge Gumbe, Fernando Alvim, António Gomes Gonga, and Álvaro Macieira.

Many Angolan artists are self-trained and have no formal education or specialized training in art. For instance, the noted painter of contemporary and modern art who produced many of Angola's postage stamps, Augusto de Andrade, is a self-taught artist. Many craftsmen are products of family apprenticeship or trained by local artists.

Some artists are, however, well trained and are graduates of art colleges. Professional training is available locally in a few art institutions such as Luanda's National School of Plastic Arts (Escola Nacional de Artes Plásticas), the National Institute for Artistic and Cultural Training, the Oliveira Salazar Industrial School, and the School of Arts, Media and Painting. Many artists are foreign trained, however, and graduate from institutions in other African as well as Latin American and European countries. On occasions, training in the form of workshops is also provided by professional artists' organizations.

Work conditions for Angolan artists are far from ideal. During the civil war, art was neglected, and existing cultural infrastructures crumbled. Although cultural development has gained momentum since the end of the war, many artists still lack the necessary facilities for their work. Most artists still work out of their homes, although some have access to studios.

A few professional organizations exist to represent artists and defend their interests. One is the Uniâo Nacional Artistas Plasticos (National Union for Plastic Artists, UNAP), organized in Benguela with another center and gallery in Luanda. Established in 1977, UNAP boasts membership that includes some of the leading Angolan artists such as Viteix and Augusto de Andrade. Other artists' groups include the Os Nacionalistas (The Nationalists), and 'Da Brigada de Jovens Artista Plásicos (Youth Brigade of Plastic Artists, BJAP). As part of their activities, these organizations hold periodic exhibits of Angolan art, particularly painting and sculpture. Through these exhibits, younger artists and their work have been promoted.

Angolan artists, especially up-and-coming ones, have had their works promoted through art competitions. One such competition designed to help expose Angola's emerging talents to the international community was held in March 2005 in Luanda and sponsored by OT Africa Line (OTAL), a leading shipping line serving western Africa. The winning entry was a painting by Manuel José Ventura, who was born in 1981. His entry was exhibited with those of other finalists in major European cities, and Ventura received a cash prize of $5,000.

Professional artists in Angola face the problem of patronage. Even though art is appreciated, most people in a society where there is rampant poverty cannot afford to expend meager resources on art. Most dealers in Angolan art and collectors of art are foreigners, particularly Europeans. Angolan art is perhaps more popular abroad than at home. Chokwe sculptures, for instance, are some of the most valued African art in Western countries and often are found on display in major art museums and galleries in Europe, the United States, and Japan.

Given the small local market, it is difficult for artists to survive solely on art production. In particular, artists working outside the areas of commercial art in Luanda and Lobito are not able to make a living from their work. Famous artist José Delgado Gomes commented on the difficulty of living solely on art:

It is difficult to keep your head above water as an artist. There is virtually no market in Angola. There are no tourists and the people are more fond of whisky than they are of art.[7]

Thus, the full-time production of art is not feasible in Angola. Most artists combine professional art with other vocations such as journalism, photography, graphic design, and the like. This is true even of highly placed artists.

Van-Dúnem, a renowned painter and holder of a graduate degree in educational art, works also as a university teacher; Álvaro Macieira, also a painter, works as a writer and a journalist and was the cultural editor of the Angolan news agency, ANGOP.

Art Galleries, Centers, and Museums

Art galleries and museums play an invaluable role in the development of Angolan visual art. During the country's long civil war, very few galleries operated. Since the cessation of hostilities, however, galleries have increasingly become important avenues for artistic appreciation. The most notable galleries are located in major cities, particularly Luanda, where there is an audience for art.

One of the earliest galleries in Angola was Galeria Humbi-Humbi in Luanda. Other galleries in the city are Galeria Cenarius, Espelho da Moda, and Galeria SOSO-Arte Contemporânea. In Luanda is also Ellinga, which is both a cultural center and an art gallery. The artists' union, UNAP, has its galleries in Luanda and Benguela. These galleries display Angolan arts from handicrafts to sculpture. Some at times host the works of foreign artists. In addition to being an avenue for displaying Angolan arts, the galleries also serve as a place for local artists to sell their work.

A number of museums also exhibit an array of Angolan arts. The Museu do Dundo (Dundo Museum) in the northeastern province of Lunda Norte has been in existence since the colonial era. It used to house one of the finest collections of Chokwe art found anywhere in the world. International art trafficking, however, has depleted this vast collection. More contemporary museums include the Museu de Angola (Museum of Angola), the Centro Cultural Português (Portuguese Cultural Center), and the Museu Nacional de História Natural (National Museum of Natural History), all located in Luanda. Local artists also own and operate a few private galleries, an example of which is Mpagar, owned by the sculptor Mpambukidi Nlunfidi.

Art Trade

The local market for art in Angola is rather limited and practically nonexistent outside the major cities. Since the end of the civil war, however, art and craft sales have increased, particularly in the tourist-industry sector, the so-called airport art. Art merchants deal in a variety of art, including antique masks, statues, paintings, fabric works, ivory, bronze, and wood carvings, and various forms of handicrafts.

The most prominent art market in Angola is the Futungo market located a few miles south of Luanda. It opens only on Sundays and caters to tourists and the Angolan expatriate community. The location of the market, close to the beautiful Luanda beaches frequented by rich Luandans and expatriates, is an impetus for its patronage. The Benfica open handicrafts market in Luanda is similarly popular. Through these markets, Angolan art has reached various parts of the world and has become popular, particularly in Europe and the Americas.

The hawking of cheap art by street vendors is also an integral part of the art market in Angola. Vendors on street corners or the major boulevards hawk anything from handicrafts to mass-reproduced paintings. A new market also has emerged, this time in cyberspace. A wave of Internet sites operated by dealers in the United States and in Europe and by some Angolan artists working abroad has widened the Angolan art trade. Some traditional Angolan art, especially masks and sculptures, may be quite expensive and run to a few thousand dollars, partly because few are produced today.

A downside of the art trade in Angola is the increasing trend toward illicit trafficking, through which the finest Angolan artworks find their way illegally to foreign lands. Reports of precious art pieces stolen from the national museum in Angola have been reported. In late 2001, the Angolan cultural services reported the theft from the museum in Dundo of a rare sixteenth-century mask of Mwana Pwo. The previous year, six Lunda-Chokwe statues were reportedly stolen from the museum of anthropology in Luanda. Rare works of art also had been stolen from the museum in Cabinda.[8]

ARCHITECTURE AND HOUSING

Angolan architecture is a mixture of the modern and the traditional. Modern, Western-style architecture is typically found in the major cities, such as the capital, Luanda, provincial administrative centers, and some coastal cities. Luanda in particular and some coastal cities such as Namibe, Benguela, and Lobito boast impressive Portuguese-style colonial buildings. In sharp contrast to the city, architecture in rural areas is simple and traditional, a reflection of the absence of modernity.

Urban Settings

The long Portuguese historical and cultural influence on Angola is evident in the architecture of urban centers. Historical buildings, particularly churches dating back to the fifteenth century, reflect Portuguese architecture. The baroque churches are generally large and generously decorated, and some have Italian marble altars.

One of the earliest churches that bears the imprint of impressive Portuguese colonial architecture is Igreja da Nossa Senhora do Cabo (Church of Our

Lady of Cabo) in Ilha de Luanda, originally build in 1575 but rebuilt in 1669. Another is a seventeenth-century Catholic church, Igreja da Nossa Senhora dos Remédios (Church of Our Lady of Remèdios), in Luanda. This church, located on Rua Rainha Ginga, was built in 1679 and has two impressive twin towers. Other churches of colonial architecture include Igreja de Jesus (Church of Jesus) at the Largo do Palacio in Cidade Alta, Igreja da Nazaré (Church of Nazarene) on the Praça do Ambiente, Igreja da Se (Church of Se) in the city of Kongo in Zaire Province, and Igreja da Sao Tiago (Church of Sao Tiago) in Namibe. These churches still retain Portuguese architecture even though renovations have been carried out over the years.

Also still bearing the mark of Portuguese colonial architecture is the Banco Nacional de Angola (National Bank of Angola) building designed by the architect Vasco Regalieira and dedicated in 1956 by Fransisco Craveiro Lopes, Portugal's president. The enormous domed pink-rose building is one of the finest examples of Portuguese colonial architecture in Angola.

In addition to colonial-style architecture, many buildings in the major cities are modern in structure, fashioned in the European style with some local adaptations. Luanda, as the nation's capital and main commercial, industrial, and port center, has many imposing modern buildings that could be found in any major Western city. In the downtown area are a number of skyscrap-

High-rising urban housing, its windows dotted with satellite dishes. However, not may people have access to satellite television as it is very expensive. Courtesy of Armando J. Rodriguez, Jr.

Modern urban architecture; in the middle of the picture is the five-star Hotel Alvalade in Luanda. Courtesy of Armando J. Rodriguez, Jr.

ers and other high-rise buildings. Usually, modern buildings are restaurants, hotels, museums, apartment complexes, educational institutions, government complexes, and churches.

The urban residential arrangement is based on socioeconomic status. This is clearly evident in a city like Luanda, where a marked contrast exists in the living conditions between the few rich and the vast poor. Typical of higher income residential neighborhoods are modern, concrete-block bungalows or multistory buildings with balconies and verandas. The houses are often big, roomy, plush, and beautifully designed, although some are less imposing. Some homes are tailored along Portuguese architecture in the residential areas. Some are actually old colonial villas deserted by Portuguese officials when Angola attained independence in 1975. Most homes are walled to deter intruders and thieves.

The majority of the population in large cities live in sprawling, unplanned, poor, and congested *bairros* (neighborhoods). Inhabitants of these poverty-ridden neighborhoods are often war refugees or internally displaced people who migrated from the rural or war-ravaged areas to eek out a living in the cities away from the devastation of the civil war. Housing in these underclass neighborhoods has distinct architecture different from that of the more

A modern home in an urban center. The slate roof and the veranda with potted plants demonstrate middle-class status usually derived from high level of educational attainment. Courtesy of Armando J. Rodriguez, Jr.

affluent districts. For instance, typical of suburban shanties such as Sambizanga district of Luanda is *musséques* architecture.

The *musséques* is a community of the very poor where hundreds of thousands of people live in crowded environments without modern amenities and basic utilities and services such as paved roads, electricity, running water, sewage and garbage disposal, and other sanitation facilities. The emergence of the *musséques* predated Angola's independence in 1975 but expanded in the war years when Luanda's population exploded because of population movements from war-affected areas.

The structures in the *musséques* consist of rundown, makeshift *cubatas* (houses) made of mud, cardboard, scrap metal, plastic sheeting, or any other available material. In the *musséques,* there is no indoor toilet, and residents rely on outdoor latrines in makeshift structures that lack modern toilet facilities.

Often, *musséques* residents introduce little improvements here and there to their shacks. In some cases, mud or even concrete blocks have replaced makeshift walls made of scrap wood or other similar materials. In other cases, corrugated, rusty tin sheets have replaced some form of temporary roofing even if the new metal roof is uneven and does not offer effective protection against rain.[9]

Angola's architectural landscape is also dotted with monuments and stat-ues, most found in Luanda. A popular monument is a bronze sculpture in Luanda, the "Monumentos das Heroínas," which immortalizes women and the role they played in the Angolan War of Independence. After indepen-dence, Angola adopted a Marxist ideology and the government erected mon-uments and statues of local heroes reminiscent of those found in Communist states like the old Soviet Union. Indeed, some of the statues were erected by Communist North Korean firms. One of the most popular monuments is that of Agostinho Neto, civil war hero and the first president of independent Angola.

Rural Architecture

Large populations in Angola live in rural areas in farm villages and hamlets. Traditional housing in rural settings made up of people of low socioeconomic status are significantly different from those of urban centers.

Common in farm villages are homesteads or huts made of mud and roofed with raffia. Sometimes, a few people who can afford it put up larger and more elaborate mud buildings or even concrete-block ones roofed with tin sheets. Generally, the village comprises many family compounds, each having

Mud-brick houses typical of rural architecture. Some are cement plastered and roofed with corrugated iron-sheets. Untarred roads that become muddy during rain also define rural set-ting. Courtesy of Armando J. Rodriguez, Jr.

a number of huts. These compounds have separate huts for the male head of the household and for each wife and her children if it is a polygynous family system. Other structures, as in the Umbundu compound, may serve as a parlor *(onjango)* for hosting guests, a kitchen *(ociwo)* for cooking and eating, a barn *(osila)* for storage purposes, a shed for keeping animals, and the spirit hut *(etambo)*. The huts in a compound are often arranged in a circular fashion called *kuimbo* among the Ngangela. In the center of this circular compound is an open playground for children and for evening or night-time leisure. Compounds are more often fenced, not so much for protection against thieves but more to prevent animals like fowl from wandering away.

House Adornment

Both in urban and rural areas, house painting and adornment is practiced. Residential houses in the cities and towns are often painted on both interior and exterior. Paint color depends on taste; some houses may be painted in bright acrylic colors, whereas others are painted in less brilliant colors.

In rural areas, the exterior walls of mud houses may be painted with decorations of geometric patterns that may hold particular meaning to the occupants or mere aesthetic value. Artistic painting of walls is common among the Lunda, and this has its origins in the people's tradition of sand drawings.[10]

The Civil War and Architecture

As to be expected, the long civil war has had a devastating effect on Angolan architecture. The ravages of the war are seen in the partial or total destruction of numerous buildings as a result of shelling and bombing. The destruction in Huambo is a testimony to the war's devastating effect on Angola's architectural infrastructure. Some of the wrecked buildings represented the best of Portuguese architecture.

The civil war not only affected urban architecture, but rural areas saw its severe impact as well. Villages were completely destroyed, particularly throughout central Angola. The destruction of village homesteads forced many people to flee into the bush or to camps consisting of makeshift structures for the displaced population.

Since the end of the war, however, bold efforts have been made to rebuild Angola's infrastructure. Shell-scarred buildings are being renovated, and building projects that were abandoned during the war are being completed. The determination to restore Angola's architectural dignity was underscored when in January 2005, Minister of Culture Boaventura Cardoso called for special attention to the restoration of monuments and historic sites in Angola.[11] In the villages, nongovernmental organizations such as Oxfam GB, which has an interest in development projects in underdeveloped areas, are assisting in the task or rebuilding.

NOTES

1. Crowley, "An African Aesthetic," 523.

2. Bastin, "Chokwe Arts," 14.

3. For discussions on Angolan art, see Wallace and Sinclair, *Art from the Frontline;* and Gillon, *Collecting African Art.*

4. For more on Chockwe art, see Bastin, *Les Sculptures Tshokwe;* and "Plates," in Jordán, *Chokwe!,* 1–55.

5. For a discussion of Chokwe sculptures with particular reference to Ilunga, see Bastin, "Statuettes Tshokwe du Héros Civilisateur Tshibinda Ilunga." For what the editor describes as a "panoramic overview of Chokwe arts," see Bastin, "Chokwe Arts," 13–19.

6. It is interesting to note that studies have explored the mathematical implications of sand drawing or its use in mathematics. See, for instance, Gerdes, *Geometry from Africa.*

7. Cited in Inge Ruigrok, "Art in the 'New' Angola."

8. For such reports, see "Angolan Artifact Stolen."

9. These works provide insight into life in the *musséques:* Monteiro, "From Extended to Residual Family"; and Moorman, "Dueling Bands and Good Girls."

10. For more on Lunda house painting, see Redinha, *Paredes Pintadas da Lunda.*

11. See "Minister of Culture Calls for Restoration of Monuments and Sites," in Republic of Angola, *Newsletter of the Embassy of Angola in the UK* (no. 101).

5

Leisure, Dress, and Cuisine

LEISURE ACTIVITIES, modes of dress, and cuisine are important elements of a people's culture and identity. In Angola during a new postwar era of peace and tranquility, leisure has once again become a national mania. The rich culture of the Angolan people also allows for a variety of dress types, from formal and ceremonial to casual and everyday wear. Also, a great variety of food types define the rich cuisine of Angola. Traditional African dishes abound and are more popular among Angolans. Some European dishes, particularly Portuguese, are served among the elite or in the expatriate community in places like Luanda, Benguela, Lobito, and Cabinda.

LEISURE ACTIVITIES

Leisure activities abound in Angola and have deep roots in the culture of the people. Among rural dwellers, traditional forms of leisure are more common. Modern forms of leisure also abound and are particularly popular with the urban population.

Traditional Leisure Forms

Rural communities still retain many of the old ways of relaxation. For instance, village pastimes for children include the traditional moonlight storytelling by elderly family members, particularly men. The evening is an occasion for older men to gather together in twos and threes or in larger groups under the shade of the tree to drink local gin, discuss a whole range of issues, or play the traditional *mancala* game. *Mancala* refers to a wooden board game, sometimes called sowing game, popular in many African societies. The game is typically played by two people on a board that varies in size from place to place. Generally, the playing board is made up of two rows, each lined with six holes, and a wider storage hole at both ends of the board. The game requires counting ability, intelligence, smart moves, and is played by moving seeds (or stones) along the pits with the aim of capturing all the opponent's seeds. *Mancala* games played in Angola include varieties known among different groups as *Kiela, owela, muvalavala, tchela, lueli, mwendo, quendo, uela, gango, biri,* and *déqui. Mancala* is so popular in Angola that *Prémio Kiela* (Kiela Prize), a championship, has been instituted for the game with winning prizes up to $1,500.[1] While the men indulge in the activities above, women may while away the time doing each other's hair, knitting, or just talking.

Festivals are still very much cherished and anticipated as leisure time by both old and young. Colorfully dressed masquerade dancers at village festivals or traditional rituals provide added entertainment. Ceremonies such as childbirth and namings, initiations, engagements, marriages, and the funerals of aged people also offer leisure opportunities. Such ceremonies are often elaborate and accompanied by recreational activities like dancing, singing, eating, drinking, and talk.

Leisure in Modern Society

The people of Angola indulge themselves in various leisure activities, whether they are rural or urban dwellers and irrespective of their socioeconomic status. For Angolans, like any other people, leisure is a way to relax and enjoy life, relieve stress, and escape the drabness of daily life. Urbanization and modernization have not obliterated the traditional forms of leisure activities. In modern urban settings, celebrations, social outings, and courtesy visits are also popular and provide important opportunities for socialization. Well-to-do people with the financial wherewithal often seize every opportunity to throw elaborate, lavish, and sometimes all-night parties. Such parties are thrown to mark milestone birthdays like the 40th, 50th, 60th, and 70th; the celebration of a child's graduation from university; the purchase of a new car; and the completion of a new house. When such parties are announced, they are anticipated by family members, friends, neighbors, acquaintances, and well-wishers.

Other leisure activities are more readily identified with urban populations. These vary from the simple and inexpensive to the more specialized. The simple, for instance, may be a leisurely evening stroll along Luanda's bay or downtown sightseeing to view the city's impressive colonial architecture. On the other hand, recreational sports like scuba diving and surfing require some expertise and quite expensive equipment.

Sports

Various types of sports have become common pastimes for most Angolans. One of the most popular sports in the country is basketball, and its games usually draw large crowds of spectators. Angolans religiously follow basketball games, whether international, national, or local. The popularity of the game emanates from Angola's highly successful basketball team, which has for many years, even during the civil war, been one of the best in Africa. It has won the prestigious African championship cup a number of times. In 2005, the team demonstrated its supremacy again when it won the coveted cup. The team also has competed in world-class championships such as those held in El Ferrol, Spain, in 1986, Argentina in 1990, and Canada in 1994. The enthusiasm for basketball in Angola and the quality of its team undoubtedly helped the country win the right to host the 2007 African championship.

Although the Angolan national soccer team has not achieved the level of success attained by its national basketball team, soccer is incredibly popular in the country and is the national sport. National soccer is organized by the Federação Angolana de Futebol (Angolan Football Federation), which

Soccer is incredibly popular in Angola, played by young people everywhere space permits. The national team, the "Black Antelopes" qualified for the 2006 FIFA World Cup, making its debut in the competition played in Germany. The team returned to a hero's welcome in Luanda, even though it did not advance beyond the first round of the competition. Courtesy of Armando J. Rodriguez, Jr.

manages the national team. In October 2005 the national team, *Palancas Negras* (Black Antelopes), did Angola proud by qualifying for the Soccer World Cup finals for the first time. In the subsequent championship played in Germany in June 2006, the team won only one game before bowing out. Nevertheless, the team returned home to a hero's welcome.

Large crowds often gather in stadiums such as Citadela Stadium in Luanda to enjoy an evening of soccer. Indeed, soccer has become a national mania, pulling crowds largely of men, but also often of women, old and young. Soccer is so popular that it is played not only on a traditional soccer pitch but also almost anywhere space and terrain allow.

Although important soccer matches like those involving the national team are always well attended, it is not uncommon to find large crowds of soccer enthusiasts at any organized game, even local ones. Thus high school tournaments are always well attended. Among youngsters, soccer is one of the most popular pastimes. Boys of school age play soccer during any free time at school and in neighborhood open spaces.

In addition to sports such as basketball and soccer, which are capable of drawing crowds of thousands at important matches, other sports provide leisure for Angolans. Many Angolans indulge themselves in watching sports like athletics (track and field), table and lawn tennis, golf, squash, hockey, volleyball, and handball. For some people, activities such as bicycling, horseback riding, aerobics and fitness, martial arts, boating, game fishing, and scuba diving are recreational. Few people, however, except wealthy Angolans and expatriates have access to many of these leisure activities. Often, they are exclusive to certain communities, and access to them requires exorbitant membership fees.

For many people, merely sharing their ideas and views with others about particular sporting events is a pastime. Games, particularly soccer, are discussed on the streets, in cafés and restaurants, and even at work. Sometimes, a victory by a favorite team or by the national team is celebrated in a carnival-like manner. For instance, the *Palancas Negras* returned from its World Cup debut to a rousing, weeklong reception by a crowd of about 50,000 Luandans and a ceremony attended by President dos Santos.

Swimming and Beach Activities

Swimming is another popular recreational activity in Angola. Even though public swimming pools are not readily available in many places, particularly in rural areas, people still enjoy swimming in rivers and streams. Swimming pools are more common in hotels, restaurants, and some exclusive clubs, but they are often available to guests only. Some public places have swimming facilities open to the public.

Angolan beaches provide better opportunity for recreational swimming and other beach activities. The country has many beautiful beaches along the coastal provinces in the west. Beach going is an important leisure activity, particularly in coastal cities such as Luanda, Benguela, Lobito, and Namibe, which have easy access to the Atlantic. Some of the most popular beaches are found around Luanda, with Ilha de Luanda and Ilha de Mussulo boasting the most impressive ones. The long, palm-dotted Palmeirinhas beach and Santiago beach south and north of Luanda, respectively, are also magnificent. The beach at Cabo Ledo, farther south on the Atlantic, is fast becoming popular for surfing. Benguela Province also has some of the best beaches in the country, such as Caota, Caotinha, Baía-Azul, and Baía-Farta.

In addition to swimming, the major beach leisure activity, Angolan beaches offer opportunities for relaxation, sunbathing, picnics, and sightseeing. Other pastimes enjoyed by many beachgoers include fishing, scuba diving, and surfing. Surfing in particular is becoming an important beach recreation and is mostly indulged in by expatriates but is increasingly becoming popular with Angolans.

Markets

Angola has many open-air street markets, some incredibly large with rich displays and a wide variety of merchandise. Such markets have become an attraction for leisure, drawing large crowds to shop and to savor the array of wares, from impressive wooden masks to assorted fabrics. For many Angolans, visiting such markets has become an important outdoor activity and pastime. A major market like Roque Santeiro in Luanda has extensive displays of a wide range of merchandise offered by thousands of vendors. Others are smaller, like Mercado São Paulo, Mercado do Kinaxixe, and Merado do Prenda. At times, some markets have added attractions. For example, the Futungo arts and crafts market near Luanda, by virtue of its proximity to the beach, is also a weekend favorite for many people. Often local musicians perform traditional music.

Cinema and Theater

Cinema going is an important and popular pastime in Angola and has become much more so since the conclusion of the civil war in 2002. During the war, the film industry suffered from neglect, and movie going followed suit. For example, Luanda's popular movie houses, such as the Karl Marx Cinema, the First of May Cinema, and the National Theater, fell into disuse. The situation has improved significantly in recent years, however. The major cities and towns boast at least one movie theater. Although the opportunity to see movies is still not readily available to many rural people because of a lack of cinema houses in villages, some rural areas sometimes have access to movies through touring mobile cinemas. Movie going is generally more popular among the young, who indulge in this pastime mostly during weekends.

Cinemagoers often have few choices in the films they can see in movie houses. Before independence, a number of revolutionary documentaries, the so-called guerrilla-films with the theme of national liberation, were produced. Angolans mostly have been bombarded with foreign films with Portuguese subtitles; in the 1990s, kung-fu movies were especially popular in the country. Because the local film industry is relatively underdeveloped, however, there has been a real lack of local film productions. The proliferation of cheap, pirated films in the 1990s as a result of the liberalization of video distribution also did a lot of damage to the indigenous film industry and discouraged theater attendance.

The situation is gradually changing in the postwar period as the Angolan film industry begins to make strides. The industry received a boost in 2004 when three movies were produced. The most important of these was Zezé Gamboa's award-winning film *o Herói* (The Hero). An inspiring movie about postwar reconstruction in Angola, *o Herói* won a number of awards, including the 2005 Sundance Film Festival's World Cinema Grand Jury Prize and the Best Feature Film award at the Pan African Film Festival in Los Angeles. The other two films produced in 2004 were *Comboio da Canhoca* (The Train of Canhoca), by Orlando Fortunato de Oliveira, and *Na Cidade Vazia* (In the Empty City), by Maria João Ganga. Thus Angolan-directed films are increasingly becoming available to moviegoers.[2]

Nowadays, cinemas do more than show films. For instance, Luanda's popular cinemas, the Karl Marx, the Tropical, and Atlântico, have hosted a number of cultural-musical performances. In October 2003, U.S. rock artist Tracy Chapman performed at the Karl Marx and the Tropical.[3]

Although cinema going is fast becoming more popular, video clubs in many cities have provided alternative sources of entertainment. Video rental clubs offer a variety of titles, mostly in Portuguese, French, and English. Low-quality, often badly dubbed videos are also available for purchase in a number of stores.

Media Entertainment

The media are also an important source of entertainment for many Angolans. Television stations feature locally produced entertainment programs, documentaries, musical videos, and films. Foreign movies and soap operas from countries like Portugal, Brazil, and the United States also feature prominently on television. Popular U.S. movies and movie stars are also quite well known in Angola. For instance, Angolans are familiar with

Arnold Schwarzenegger, Jack Nicholson, and Woody Allen. Satellite dishes are becoming more prominent in urban areas, and this has given more people access to a greater variety of films. Television also offers an avenue through which many people watch soccer and other games.

Angolans also pass the time listening to radio, which is more readily available to people. Like television, radio offers a variety of entertainment programs and music. Although commercial radio broadcasts contain local content, much of it is foreign, particularly Portuguese and U.S.

A less popular form of leisure is performing theater because the Angolan theater industry has not been very active.[4] This is partly due to lack of infrastructure and institutional support to engender sustained production. The elite classes of the cities, however, occasionally see plays performed by foreign and local groups in places like the National Theatre in Luanda and the newly opened Agostinho Neto cultural center. Occasional concerts featuring talented Angolan artists are also held at major theaters such the Karl Marx and in smaller venues around the major cities.

Tourists Attractions

Angola is a country of rich in tourist attractions, although the growth of tourism has been severely stunted by the civil war. The varieties of tourist attractions provide leisure opportunities to many people. Among the most popular places frequented by Luandans and tourists are the wide, sandy beaches of the Ilha do Mussulo. Lined with coconut palms, the beautiful beaches provide a peaceful atmosphere for various kinds of leisure activities from swimming and sunbathing to fishing and surfing. Some beaches like those of Ilha de Luanda have resort centers that provide leisure facilities such as bungalows, restaurants, and bars. The beaches serve as exciting weekend getaway spots for those who can afford the expense.

Museums and galleries also provide Angolans avenues for leisure. One of the most popular museums frequented by tourists is Museu da Escravatura (Museum of Slavery), located south of Luanda along the coast on top of a hill overlooking the beach. The museum, housed in a white building, is supposedly located at the point where African captives were kept before being shipped to New World destinations through the infamous Middle Passage. The museum preserves the history of the Atlantic slave trade on the Angolan coast.

Another important attraction is the Museu Nacional de Antropologia (National Anthropology Museum) in Luanda, a popular place for lovers of art and crafts. Here, visitors may savor an impressive collection of African arts. The Humbi-Humbi art gallery also provides an opportunity to appreciate art. Also popular in Luanda is the Museum of Natural History, which houses exhibits of Angola's marine life. The Military Museum in Luanda, in a historic fortress, is also a popular attraction.

Wildlife and parks also offer Angolans leisure. Efforts have been made to preserve wildlife threatened with extinction and protect exotic birds and plants through a system of parks and reserves. National parks and reserves dot the country and include Kwando and Cangandala (Malange Province), Kameia (Moxico Province), Bicuar (Huíla Province), Mupa (Cunene Province), and Iona (Namibe Province).

The most prominent of the Angolan national parks is the Kissama National Park located about 45 miles south of Luanda. Despite the civil war and the decimation of wildlife in Angola as a result of poaching, the park remains famous for its different kinds of animals such as lions, giraffes, buffalo, antelope, elephants, boars, rhinos, and many others. The park also provides leisure activities such as hiking, sightseeing, camping, picnicking, guided tours, and boat trips. Good hotel accommodations in the form of bungalow huts with standard amenities such as bathroom, double bed, and television are also available in the park.

As a land of panoramic natural beauty, Angola has many magnificent natural landscapes such as waterfalls and rock formations that have become sources of recreation to many people, particularly tourists. In Malange Province, on the Lucala River near the north-central city of Malange, is a spectacular waterfall, the Kalandula (formerly known as Duque de Braganca falls). Tumbling more than 300 feet, the massive waterfalls are a truly an impressive sight. Also in Malange Province are the giant Black Rocks at Pungo Andongo. The rocks are a range of spectacular natural formations in the shape of animals and are an inviting recreational location. Each of these enormous rocks is about 300 feet tall.

Nightlife

Urban Angolans often enjoy themselves with a night out at restaurants, nightclubs, cafés, and bars, where people while away the time talking, drinking, dancing, and generally socializing. Many city dwellers love to frequent these spots, which Angolan cities offer in abundance. In Luanda, some downtown restaurants are rather expensive, serving international dishes and frequented mainly by wealthy Angolans and expatriates. Others places that serve local dishes exclusively are less expensive. At makeshift roadside food courts women serve local dishes and alcoholic beverages; their customers include locals as well as people from the expatriate community.

Nightclubs have become popular in postwar Angola. Some hotels such as Luanda's Hotel Continental and Hotel Panorama have nightclubs. More popular are the numerous independent nightclubs in the big cities.

Some of Luanda's popular clubs are Balumuka, Pub la bamba Boite, Cafe Paris, Cenarius, Contencioso, Don Quixote, Havana Café, Paralelo 2000, Tambarino, Teatro Avenida, and Xavarotti.

Nightlife in Angola flourishes more during weekends than on weekdays, and many nightclubs remain open until the early hours of the morning. Nightclubs usually have bars that sell different kinds of alcoholic drinks, from locally brewed beers to expensive imported wines. Drinking, indeed, is a popular nightclub pastime, and there is no enforceable official age restriction to consumption of alcohol. Most clubs have discotheques where disc jockeys mix recorded popular Western music, particularly U.S. hip-hop hits, for the enjoyment of enthusiastic pub crawlers. A few clubs occasionally offer live music played by local professional or amateur bands. Apart from drinking, for many who attend nightclubs, the dance floor is the real attraction, and dancing may last until the early hours of the morning.

Men generally have greater freedom than women to frequent nightclubs and indulge in the nightlife. Women are restricted by social and cultural values to indulge in such pastimes. A woman visiting a nightclub bar is likely to be looked upon as loose or unrespectable. Young urban women, however, find it easier to break social and cultural taboos and may be found in nightclubs. For young men and women, the nightclubs increasingly provide opportunities for rendezvous.

Although Luanda has an intense nightlife, as do other places, it has its own drawbacks. Some pubs, especially the low-quality ones in dark alleys, are also used as joints for prostitution, even involving underage girls. Also, excessive alcohol consumption causes all kinds of trouble, such as brawls, thieving, muggings, and more serious criminal activities.

Work-free days such as public and religious holidays are always occasions for leisure activities. Angolans use holidays to throw parties, go on picnics and safaris, go sightseeing, and visit beaches and other recreational areas. The Yuletide season, from Christmas Eve to New Year's Day, is one of the most important periods for festivities. This is often a week of junketing when various social, ethnic, and cultural groups hold annual parties and when family members get together for reunions and merriment accompanied by food and drink. Independence Day, November 11, is also an occasion for celebration and has become more so since the end of the civil war.

DRESS

The culture of Angola is greatly enriched by its dress tradition. Dress comes in different styles, designs, and in assorted materials. Dress is a depiction of individual character, and the way a person dresses especially in formal settings goes a long way to define his or her social status in society, level of education, religion, and marital status. What an individual wears also suggests age; the older people tend to dress more conservatively than the younger ones. Yet dress is also a cultural expression of ethnolinguistic identity. Many ethnic groups are identified with particular forms of traditional attire peculiar to them.

Dress in the context of Angola's culture includes the clothing items that an individual puts on, from cap (for a man) or head tie (for a woman) to shoes. Dress also includes the various ways by which people adorn the body, such as the use of jewelry and other ornamentation. Dress, in effect, is the totality of the appearance of the person.

Traditional Dress

Traditional dress still retains its cultural importance in modern Angola despite the predominance of Western clothing. Generally, traditional Angolan attire is made from hand-woven cotton fabrics, although animal skinwear is known among some groups. A blouse worn over wrap-around cloth covering the torso and completed with a head tie is typical for women.

Body adornment is important in traditional dress. Elaborate body decoration and scarification have always been a rich part of the culture of Angolans. For men, body adornment in the form of tattoos is rooted in the culture, sometimes representing social status and prestige. Tattoos may also sometimes be worn for celebrating traditional festivals or participating in certain rituals and rites as required by custom.

Adornment for ritual purposes is not peculiar to men; young girls undergoing puberty rites or priestesses may wear chalk or charcoal body marks. More importantly for women and young girls, however, body adornment is principally an expression of beauty. Women adorn themselves with different types of elaborate hairstyles. In addition to weaving, the hair may also be decorated with various objects such as beads and braided extensions hanging down the neck to the shoulder. Also, part of women's dress is the wearing of locally made shell necklaces, bracelets, anklets, and beads.

One form of traditional dress is the different ceremonial garb worn during cultural festivals and ceremonies such as initiation rites. For instance, *makishi* masqueraders wear a great variety of complex attire during *mukanda* rites of passage. The *makishi* attire is made up of different materials depending on the particular culture. Generally, the body costume from the shoulders down is made of woven vegetable fiber or beaten bark. The mask is made of elaborately designed wood or resin.

The attire of royalty is more elaborate than that of commoners. Among the Lunda, chiefly ceremonial regalia consist of brightly decorated midlength

Women in various casual traditional wears. Courtesy of Armando J. Rodriguez, Jr.

skirt dresses completed with crowns of various prestige, depending on chiefly status.

Although Angolans have a rich dress culture that has been significantly modernized, some remote rural communities have resisted change in their form of dress and have stuck to their ancient ways of dressing. This is true of the Ovahimba, a seminomadic pastoral people of southern Angola (and also of northern Namibia). These people have retained the old ways; their women still go bare breasted, and they coat their bodies with red ocher and fat as protection against the sweltering desert sun. Also, they wear long braided hair similarly coated with the ocher mixture.

Western Fashion

Western clothing and European dress have a long history in Angola, dating to colonial times. In colonial Angola, Christian missionaries and the Portuguese colonial policy of assimilation strongly discouraged African culture, regarding it as uncivilized. For the African, therefore, to be educated and civilized partly meant abandoning African dress for the European style. The popularity of Western clothing in modern Angola is a product of Portuguese colonial and missionary influences.

Western clothing today is not only very popular in urban centers but also in the villages. In practically every corner of the country, Western clothing,

Young people generally wear Western, casual clothing like T-shirts. Courtesy of Armando J. Rodriguez, Jr.

as one would find in any Western city, is the most common mode of dressing on a daily basis and on most occasions. Women's causal wear includes blouses and skirts, whereas men's is T-shirts over trousers or shorts. Among the youth, both women and men, blue jeans are very popular.

Although casual wear is appropriate at most times and on informal social outings, Westernized Angolans dress more formally for official and formal occasions such as weddings. Women wear dresses, sometimes with hats; men wear suits or blazers and trousers with shirts with ties. Local cultures in many places frown at immodest dress and clothing that reveals intimate body parts, breasts, for instance, on the part of women. Although older women and those in rural areas are more conservative in their manner of dress, it is common in more morally relaxed urban areas to find young girls in provocative, skimpy, and revealing clothing, such as tight miniskirts.

Body decoration and adornment are still part of modern dress in Angola. Both men and women display wealth by sporting expensive ornaments such as wristwatches and jewelry to match their clothing. Women consider the wearing of cosmetics and perfumes, necklaces, trinkets, pendants, and other body ornaments as complements to their beauty.

Whatever the manner of dress, Angolans generally take great pride in their appearance. Many people are not able to dress in expensive clothing, but neatness is emphasized. Certain categories of people are required to wear uniforms by the virtue of their occupations. For instance, members of the armed forces, the police, immigration officers, and firefighters are in state-prescribed uniforms during their official duties. Certain hospital workers such as nurses and maids are also required to wear uniforms. Also, students up to postprimary level wear school uniforms that differ from school to school.

Clothing and Fashion

The clothing and fashion industry in Angola is not well developed. Many local tailors serve their immediate communities, but very few modern fashion designers and creators exist. Major cities such as Luanda have a few small boutiques that sell cloth, shoes, bags, and other items imported from Portugal, the United States, France, Italy, South Africa, and other foreign counties. Locally made cloths are available, but they are often of low quality. Clothing items and other paraphernalia are often quite expensive. This is due mainly to the lack of necessary materials for manufacturing. Although in the 1970s Angola exported cotton, today the textile industry is forced to turn to other African countries to obtain necessary materials for production.

A proud Angolan displaying his cap decorated with the national colors of bright red and black. Courtesy of Armando J. Rodriguez, Jr.

CUISINE

Angolan cuisine includes a variety of traditional dishes, many of which have been influenced by foreign food culture. As a Portuguese colony, Angola's national cuisine is particularly influenced by the erstwhile colonial power. During the colonial period, Portuguese immigrants to Angola bought their cuisine and cooking habits, and these have greatly impacted Angolan cuisine.

Angola's staple foods often consist of flour, beans, and rice with meat, fish, chicken, and different kinds of sauces. Vegetables are an important component of the Angolan diet. Sweet potato leaves, tomatoes, onions, and okra accompany other dishes or are ingredients in their preparation. The people of Angola also like to season their food with different types of spices such as garlic. Angolan cuisine is thus very tasty and richly flavored.

Cooking of meals in the open is common particularly in rural areas. Courtesy of Armando J. Rodriguez, Jr.

Types of Dishes

Many popular dishes may be counted as part of the national cuisine. Fish dishes are very common, such as *calulu,* which is made out of dried and fresh fish accompanied by sweet potato leaves and sliced okra. This dish may be served with palm oil beans or *funge,* a popular corn flour pudding. Another fish dish is *mufete de cacuso,* made with grilled tilapia. This is also served with palm oil beans and cooked manioc. Also popular are chicken dishes such as *muamba,* a pepper- and garlic-seasoned chicken dish often served with palm oil beans or *funge.*[5]

Beverages

Angolan cuisine includes beverages, both soft and alcoholic. Popular soft drinks include Coca-Cola, Pepsi, Mirinda, Sprite, and Fanta. Some soft drinks are imported from neighboring states such as South Africa and Namibia and faraway countries like Brazil and Portugal. Since the end of the civil war, however, the Angolan soft-drink industry has steadily increased its production capacity. Improvements have been made to the manufacturing infrastructure, and in recent years, large-scale investments have been made in the soft-drink industry by multinational corporations. In 2000, Coca-Cola opened a plant at Bom Jesus in Bengo Province, an investment of about $36 million. A second Coca-Cola plant also has opened in the southern city of Lubango.

Soft drinks are served on almost all occasions, such as parties and celebrations. In addition to soft drinks, hosts of such occasions might also provide beer for those interested. Beer, however, is consumed more often in pubs and clubs. The Angolan beer industry is controlled by Empresa Angolana de Cerveja (EKA) and Nova Empresa de Cerveja de Angola (NOCAL). Big hotels and high-class restaurants that have many international visitors also feature extensive lists of foreign wines.

For those who cannot afford the expensive beer and imported wine, locally brewed beverages such as maize beer, palm wine *(maluvu),* and corn-flour drink *(kissangua* or *ocissangua)* are available. A popular local alcoholic drink is *caxi,* which is distilled from cassava and potato skins. Mongozo is another traditional beer made from palm nuts, which had been brewed by the Chokwe people prior to the arrival of Europeans. Although still brewed locally, the production has been modernized and Mongozo marketed in some parts of Europe, particularly in Belgium where it is produced by Van Steenberge. The entry of Mongozo into the international beer market is a result of the enterprising efforts of Henrique Kabia, an Angolan living in Belgium. In adopting modern methods of brewing, Kabia has retained the original traditional African recipe so that the original taste is preserved.

In the traditional society, alcoholic beverages like Mongozo are consumed from a calabash (gourd). It is generally believed that the use of a calabash preserves the authentic taste and flavor of a drink and its freshness. Even though glass cups are available, many people prefer to use a calabash. In some modern settings like pubs and restaurants, it is fashionable to drink local beer from calabashes.

Patterns of Consumption

Home cooking is a strong tradition among Angolans, and the practice of eating out is not particularly encouraged. Foodstuffs can be purchased at the many indoor or open markets in almost every town and city. Practically everything is available, from meat to baby food. In addition to the local markets, there are big, modern supermarkets in urban centers where frozen food, imported wine, and the like may be purchased. Supermarkets are more popular with the elite and expatriates.

Although Angolans cherish home-cooked food, many people, usually in the urban areas, spend leisure time in restaurants. Numerous small, local restaurants serve exclusively traditional Angolan dishes. A few high-class restaurants, especially in the major cities, specialize in international cuisines, including Portuguese, Spanish, Italian, Swedish, and Brazilian. In Luanda, some of the most impressive restaurants are located on the Ilha. A few restaurants in Angola, such as Chez Wou and Restaurant Tam 8, Chinese and Vietnamese restaurants, respectively, in Luanda, provide ethnic food. Some restaurants specialize in particular foods, such as Fish Paradiso, a seafood restaurant. Luanda's top restaurants, such as Afrodisiakus, Clube de Empresarios, and Farol Velho, are well equipped and have indoor and outdoor dinning. Restaurants such as Pizzaria Bela Napoles offer carryout foods. Others provide lunch buffets. Most restaurants open daily for lunch and dinner, although some close on Sundays.

Parties and other celebrations organized by wealthy individuals are always occasions for large-scale cooking for invited guests, although the uninvited often show up. In such gatherings, traditional dishes as well as rice with chicken may be served. These are accompanied by drinking, either of soft drinks or beer, which are freely and liberally consumed.

Notes

1. More on *mancala* games in Angola is provided in Elísio Santos Silva, *Jogos de quadrícula do tipo mancala com especial incidência nos praticados em Angola* [*Board games of the mancala type with special attention for those played in Angola*] (Lisboa: Instituto de Investigação Científica Tropical, 1995).

2. Some analysis of the improvement in Angola's film industry is provided in Ruigrok, "Angola Cinema Flourishes after the War."

3. For a brief piece on the history of cinema in Angola, see Moorman, "Of Westerns, Women, and War."

4. For a useful source on theater in Lusophone Africa, see Mitras, "Theatre in Portuguese Speaking African Countries."

5. For some discussion of the cuisine of Angola, see Hamilton, *Cuisines of Portuguese Encounters.* See also Harris, *The Africa Cookbook;* Hultman, *The Africa News Cookbook;* and Hafner, *A Taste of Africa.*

6

Marriage, Family, and Gender Roles

Relatives are a better defense than a fortress.

—Umbundu proverb

THE INSTITUTIONS OF FAMILY and marriage and ideas about gender roles within the household and in larger society are important elements of the culture of the Angolan people. Although these practices are deeply embedded in the cultural history of Angola, long colonial occupation with its concomitant infusion of Western culture through education, religion, and social values has significantly impacted them. Traditional notions and views on marriage, family, and gender roles have seen important transformations. These transformations began to occur with the arrival of the Portuguese to south-central Africa. First the slave trade and then colonial occupation greatly affected traditional beliefs. The colonial experience was accompanied by Portuguese religious and cultural influences. Western education, Christianity, and urbanization, to a considerable extent, brought about social change.

In addition to the colonial experience, as is true of most areas of life in Angola, many years of devastating wars also have had important consequences for family and marriage institutions. For example, family dislocation has occurred on a large scale as a result of the destructive war.

These factors have, however, not totally obliterated traditional family beliefs and practices, marriage patterns, and gender roles. Angolans still cherish the family institution and kin relationships; marriage is important, the bearing of children is considered essential, and importance is placed on gender roles and division of labor.

MARRIAGE

Marriage has an important place in the culture of Angola. It is central not only to the formation of the family, but it is also a vehicle for interfamily and communal relationships and for cohesion among many ethnolinguistic groups. In traditional societies, a marriage is not only a union of two individuals but also one of two families. Sometimes, a marriage is even intended to build or cement ties between two communities or clans.

Except for those in a Roman Catholic religious order, celibacy is not considered part of life in Angola. Parents expect their children to marry and produce grandchildren. In modern times when arranged marriage is no longer in vogue, mothers in particular worry when their marriageable children, especially daughters, are not yet married. Marrying off children is considered a sign of successful parentage. Young men and women look forward to marriage.

Broadly, two types of marriages exist: the traditional and the modern. These types are discussed in following sections; suffice it to say that the traditional type is rooted in customs and practices of the different ethnolinguistic groups, whereas the modern types are a product of Western influence. In modern Angola, traditional marriage has declined, although it is still practiced in many places, particularly rural areas. Modern forms of marriage, on the other hand, are popular in urban centers.

Forms of Marriage

One of the most important characteristics of traditional marriage is that it is more often than not arranged. Marriages are arranged by family members, especially parents, and sometimes other elders. An arranged marriage is more likely based on the general mutual interests of the families, rather than on the interests of the two people involved. The marriage may be intended to establish friendship or promote existing ties, political or economic, between the two families. Love and affection for each other by the couple intending to marry are not of primary importance in arranging marriages.

In traditional marriages, girls usually marry rather young. A bride is expected to be significantly younger than her prospective husband. The age superiority on the part of the man is expected to confer on him a superior status in the marriage and within the family. In a traditional Angolan family, a woman is considered subservient to her husband.

Also, unlike in modern times, traditional marriage is more insistent on the chastity of the bride before marriage. A girl is expected to be a virgin until marriage, and the families of both the groom and the bride look forward to this proved on the wedding night. For the groom's family, evidence of the bride's virginity, symbolized by blood on the marriage bed, is an indication that their son had married a worthy woman of virtue. If virginity is not proved, it is a source of shame to the bride's family. The groom's family may demand the return of the bride-price paid on the woman. A more severe reaction is an outright annulment of the marriage.

Some traditional marriages are polygynous, in which a man has more than one wife; in fact, polygyny is encouraged among many ethnolinguistic groups. Although the Popular Movement for the Liberation of Angola (Movimento Popular de Libertação de Angola, MPLA) government banned the practice after independence, it is a cultural tradition hard to eliminate. In modern Angola, even in urban areas, polygyny is still practiced.

Western educational and religious influences have introduced significant changes into the marriage institution in Angola. In modern society, for instance, arranged marriage has significantly declined, particularly in urban areas. Young people today find their own marriage partners without parental input; although, for the most part, conjugal relationships are made with parental blessings.

Two forms of modern marriage exist, namely church marriage and civil marriage, both of which are predominant in the cities and towns compared to rural areas. A high percentage of Angolans have adopted the Christian marriage form, which is common among urbanized Angolans who are products of Western education and Euro-Christian upbringing. It is a marriage type based on the Christian tenets and principles of conjugal relationship. Roman Catholicism, to which large populations of Angolans adhere, does not permit polygyny. Christian teachings also frown on premarital sexual relations, although virginity is not often verified by most churches before agreeing to join couples in holy matrimony.

The second form of modern marriage is civil marriage, which is contracted in court under a court clerk employed by the government. The exchange of vows is conducted according to Angola's legal code of marriage. Like church marriage, the legal system in Angola does not officially recognize polygyny.

All marriage forms place great value on marital fidelity. Tradition frowns on adultery, and Christian and court marriages are guided by a code of marital faithfulness that may be a valid ground for divorce if broken. In contemporary times, however, infidelity is common, particularly in the urban areas, and society tends to be more tolerant of adultery when committed by a man than when committed by a woman.

Although homosexuals in Western nations and a few African states like South Africa are vocal about the recognition of same-sex marriage, it is not a subject for consideration in Angola. Homosexuality and same-sex marriage are illegal and are generally not culturally accepted. The International

Lesbian and Gay Associations (ILGA), a global network of homosexuals, quoted Angola's laws as depicting homosexual acts as "offences against public morality."[1] Disapproval of homosexuality in Angola seems to be in line with the belief of many Africans that it is alien to African culture.

Mention should be made of a new marriage pattern emerging in Angola, although not yet common. This is marriage among Muslims according to Islamic rites and traditions.

Marriage Procedure

Marriage procedures vary in Angola and depend on the type being conducted. Whatever kind, however, it is still customary, even in modern marriages, for a formal ceremony of introduction to be conducted. This is a rather elaborate ceremony that formally brings the two families together. It is an occasion for celebration and merriment and allows parents and elders on both sides to bestow blessings on the couple. The ceremony of introduction also offers the groom's family the opportunity to formally seek the hand of the woman in marriage for their son. Upon the acceptance of the groom's marriage request, the bride-price is then set.

Bride-price *(alambamento),* sometimes referred to as bride wealth, is an important and indispensable aspect of marriage in Angola. It is the practice whereby the groom and his family provide gifts to the bride's family. Usually, the gifts consist of clothing, livestock like cattle and goats, food items like grain, and other items. In more recent times, the bride-price has usually included money. Bride-price cements the decision of the bride's family to release their daughter in marriage to the prospective husband. Its importance in the Angolan culture is demonstrated in a 1971 Luandan bilingual musical, *bride price,* one of the first modern dramas performed in Lusophone Africa.[2]

Bride-price is an ancient practice that persists in modern Angola, even in urban places, despite social change brought about by Westernization. It is more cherished in the rural areas, however, where arranged marriages are common. Bride-price is customarily presented in a ceremony. It is also an occasion for the gathering of the two families in celebration.

In Angola, as elsewhere where bride-price is practiced, a controversy has arisen over its utility in the modern age. Culturally, bride-price is intended as an indication of the groom's sincere intention to be married and of his recognition of the bride as valuable. It also establishes an alliance between the two families. It has been argued that bride-price promotes greater commitment to the family, especially on the part of the wife. Some have argued, however, that it amounts to the purchase of the woman, which confers on the man the license to mistreat her. Thus, bride-price has been blamed for abusive behavior by men to their wives. Also, in the prevailing time of serious economic difficulties, the practice is said to provide the bride's family an opportunity to exploit the groom.

Elements of traditional marriage have been incorporated into modern marriages. The bride-price, for example, has become an integral part of modern marriage, whether church or civil marriage. It is still widely practiced in urban Angola, even among the elite.

Christian marriage is basically Western and is conducted in a church service presided over by ordained clergy. The wedding service, conducted in Portuguese or in the vernacular and sometimes in a combination of both, is colorful but solemn, consisting of hymns, scripture readings, and a sermon. The exchange of vows is conducted in line with the sacraments of holy matrimony, such as marriage sanctity and its indissolubility. Bridal dress is Western formal; the groom is required to dress in a suit with tie and shoes to match. The wedding gown and veil for the bride is white, with white shoes and a pair of white gloves to match. The bridal party and the groom's men are also brightly dressed in Western attire. After the union has been pronounced by the presiding clergy, it is symbolized by an exchange of wedding bands by the newlyweds.

Church weddings are often elaborate and, therefore, quite expensive. For Angolans who desire a less elaborate or less expensive marriage ceremony that is legally recognized, the civil wedding provides an alternative. All weddings, however, usually conclude with a lavish reception.

Marriage and Social Change

In modern society, the choice of marriage partner is no longer that of the parents, but entirely that of the individuals concerned. In other words, arranged marriages are no longer in vogue, particularly in the cities and towns. This, however, does not preclude the fact that parents still play a large role in the making of conjugal unions. In some instances, parents are still able to disapprove of prospective life partners of their children when they consider such partners unsuitable for whatever reasons.

Prescribed marriage, which is the tradition in some places, in Lunda Norte, for example, has been greatly discouraged. Prescribed marriage is when intermarriage with other ethnolinguistic groups is prohibited and a person must marry within his or her own group or even within kin or extended family. In the present dispensation, people have greater freedom to find marriage partners with whomever they fancy, irrespective of kin or group.

In the past it was common and culturally acceptable to marry girls at a rather young age, about 15 among the Ngangela, for example. Although the legal age at which a woman can marry in Angola is 15, with parental consent as a minor, underage marriage is rather common. Girls have been withdrawn from school to be given away in marriage by parents. During the civil war, there was a very high incidence of young girls forced into marriage with soldiers. The government has conducted a campaign to end early marriage for girls. In a recent visit to Cacolo district in eastern Lunda Sul Province, where underage marriage is common among the Lunda-Chokwe, Minister for Family Affairs and Woman Promotion Cândida Celeste condemned the act.[3] The government's strategy is to encourage girls' education, particularly postprimary schooling. The efforts of the government to deal with underage girls' marriage have been complemented by campaigns by social critics and child advocates. These efforts have begun to yield results.

The divorce rate has increased in Angola since independence largely because of the civil war. Not all cases, of course, can be attributed to the war. Adultery is often grounds for divorce, especially when committed by a woman. Other domestic factors include spousal abuse and neglect. In the past, divorced women or widows, particularly illiterate ones, were often denied access to family property. Advocates have promoted changes in divorce and inheritance laws to be fairer to women. In many urban places, a widow now has at least a substantial share in the wealth of her dead husband. In cases of divorce, women increasingly gain custody of the children.

FAMILY

In Angola, as in other cultures of the world, the family is a socially recognized institution consisting of members who share common values and are committed to one another. Every family has an identity through name, history, and dwelling place, though all family members may not necessarily dwell under one roof. Whether they live together of not, family members ideally work for the common good of one another.

Basically, two types of families live in Angola. These are traditional and modern, and both coexist in modern society. The traditional family is one in which a household consists of not only a man, his wife or wives, and their children but also other relatives living in the same household, or even outside it. Among many groups, such as the Bakongo, departed ancestors are regarded as part of the family, and it is believed that they should be consulted when occasion demands, such as when advice is needed on a particular issue or problem. The traditional family can thus be defined as a social unit of individuals related by common ancestry, lineage, blood, or marriage. Cousins, aunts, nephews, nieces, and grandparents are all members of the traditional family. It is most prevalent in rural societies where the traditional village structures remain in place.

The traditional family system is necessarily an extended one because it includes close and distant relatives. It thus emphasizes strong kin relationships, although the importance of such relationships might differ from one ethnic group to another. In the extended family unit, everyone is expected to lend a hand in the upbringing of children.

The traditional family is equally large because it is polygynous. Customs and culture among practically all Angolan ethnolinguistic groups permit polygyny, the practice of a man having multiple wives at the same time. Although polygyny is a socially accepted practice, polyandry, the practice in which a woman has more than one husband, is taboo.

In many parts of Angola, particularly in war-affected areas, the number of women is disproportionately greater than the number of men of marriageable age. In this situation, polygynous households tend to be predominant. Polygyny is also widely practiced in rural areas. By the late 1980s, about 20 percent of rural families were polygynous, and 40 percent of married rural women lived in polygynous homes.[4]

The extended and polygynous traditional family system has existed for centuries and is still important in many areas. In contemporary times, however, it has declined, particularly in urban areas. Modernization and social change in contemporary Angola as well as other factors account for this.

In cities and towns, extended and polygynous families exist, although not on the same scale as in the villages, and consist of extended family members and even nonrelatives who have acquired family membership by virtue of a long stay in the household. During the civil war, the devastation in the countryside forced many people to flee the villages and rural areas for the relatively safer cities. For instance, many Luandan families took in refugees and displaced individuals who further swelled the size of the families.

In traditional polygynous village families, the wives live with the man under the same roof. What is more common in the urban form of polygyny is that the other wife (or wives, as the case may be) lives separately, away from the man's household in a housing unit of her own, which may be managed by the man. The nonresident second wife is still legitimately married to the man either by customary law or by some sort of culturally accepted arrangement. Also nothing precludes the absentee wife from bearing children for her husband, just like the resident wife.

This form of polygyny in which a man's other wife (or wives) resides separately from the man's household is not legal if the man's marriage to one wife has been formally contracted by law through the courts or consecrated under Christian matrimonial tenets. Nevertheless, the lax enforcement of laws in Angola coupled with social and cultural norms have permitted men to have wives outside the household.

In modern Angola, however, the importance of the extended polygynous family has been greatly diminished. Many educated urbanized people have adopted the modern monogamous nuclear family, at least officially. The modern family consists of a man, his wife, and the children that they rear. The family, therefore, tends to be small, and the average household size is becoming smaller and often limited to six people: parents and four children.

Lineage and Social Patterns

The lineage is a unit of social organization based on kinship. All members of a lineage are descended from a common ancestor. If this ancestor is a female and the descent is through females, the unit is matrilineal. This form of social identity is known among many Angolan people, including the Bakongo, the Mbundu, the Chokwe, and the Ovambo. The matrilineal descent unit has declined in importance under the influence of colonialism and the war. In precolonial times, matrilineage coexisted with a patrilineal system in which descent is through males via a male ancestor. This double descent system was known among the Ovimbundu, among whom economic issues such as property rights and inheritance were determined through the matrilineal system and political authority through patrilineage.

IMPACT OF THE CIVIL WAR ON THE FAMILY

The civil war has had a debilitating effect on family relationships in Angola. It has severely affected the cohesion and the integrity of the family. During the war, large-scale dislocation of families occurred, mostly through destruction of villages and forced migrations for safety. Family members were displaced and scattered, in some cases never to be reunited. Reports exist of children kidnapped during the war who were unable to trace their families or places of origin.

One of the consequences of family displacement is the breakdown of cherished kinship ties, even in rural areas where they used to be strong. Communal relationships also have declined and have been replaced by growing individualism. As Inge Tvedten has commented, "women have begun charging for looking after other people's children, taking their laundry and cleaning their houses, or plaiting hair."[5] The massive deployment of land mines during the war has further contributed to the difficulty in maintaining family and communal links.

Family dislocation also has had the negative effect of bringing economic insecurity to many households. The near total collapse of the economy has been a major blow to many families in rural areas and urban slums. Many women, especially those who have become heads of households because of the absence of the husband, have had to take on greater economic responsibilities.

More have taken to farming and laboring in the fields to maintain the household.

GENDER ROLES

The family is a social structure in which important functions and tasks must be performed to ensure its well-being. Necessary functions range from economic management for physical survival to procreation for generational survival. In the Angolan household, as in most families around the world, there is shared responsibility based on gender and age.

In Angola, theoretically, men and women have equal status and rights as recognized by the constitution and other legal devices such as the Family Code. Spousal equal obligations within the family are expressed thus:

They must decide together all matrimonial questions, including the raising and education of children; both must contribute to family responsibilities and participate in domestic chores; each has the right to work professionally or engage in activities of his/her choice as long as such work and activities do nor compromise his/her obligations to the family; each has the same powers of acquisition, administration and use of all that the couple owns.[6]

In reality, however, men traditionally have been the household heads with the primary responsibility of supporting and providing for all family members. As head of the household, the man is the principal decision maker in practically all matters, although this is truer in the traditional family than in the modern urban family. The man is the main provider of financial security for the family even though in educated nuclear families the woman supplements family income by taking a job outside the home. In the modern society, one of the most important tasks of the man of the house is to see to the education of his children. The responsibility of imparting discipline to the children also falls more on the man than on the woman. Generally, the man as household head is responsible for the welfare of the family.

In the Angolan household, women play a subordinate and supportive role to their husbands, especially in matters of decision making. A woman's main responsibility to her husband is to cater to both his physical and his sexual needs. Men cherish wives who ensure that their meals are ready on time, their cloths washed, and their availability for conjugal pleasure assured whenever desired. It is also widely accepted that women have the primary task of child rearing and care. In the past in traditional homes, women were expected to bear as many children as possible. On average, a woman bore as many as six or seven children. One of the reasons for bearing many children was the high rate of infant mortality; only two or three children might survive. Also, the

Male youths often take to odd jobs like car washing as a survival strategy in a depressed economy. Courtesy of Armando J. Rodriguez, Jr.

need for helping hands on the farm in agricultural communities necessitated having many children.

In addition to child-care responsibilities, women are expected to take care of everyday domestic chores such as washing clothes, fetching firewood for cooking, and preparing meals. In rural agricultural communities, women are involved in subsistence agriculture, raising food crops for family consumption or for occasional marketing. Indeed, rural women increasingly have taken on the burden of subsistence agriculture and are responsible for producing crops such as manioc, maize (corn), beans, sorghum, sweet potato, and millet. Thus, agriculture has become an important vocation for women in many places.

These ventures go hand in hand with child care, and it is a common sight in Angola to see women, whether working on the farm in the village or selling wares in city markets, with their infants strapped on their backs while they work.

In urban areas, men and women tend to share some parental care. Both parents are responsible for the socialization of their children in the process of growing up. To a large extent, however, this responsibility still falls more on women than on men, especially in traditional polygynous households. In some instances, women have become heads of households who must run the family in the absence of a husband or the support of a man. The female-headed household has become prevalent as a result of the civil war

A young girl cares for her younger sibling, a phenomenon quite common in Angola. Courtesy of Armando J.
Rodriguez, Jr.

that caused the deaths of thousands of men and forced many others to abandon their homes through conscription. By the early 1990s, an estimated 35
percent of Angola's family units were headed by females.[7]

A surplus of women, however, does not necessarily result in female-headed
households. Tvedten has pointed out that in the late 1980s in the villages of
rural southwestern Namibe, Cunene, and southern Huíla Provinces, there
were "78.2 men per 100 women in the agricultural zone and 72.5 men per
100 women in the pastoral zone," and that in the 20–24 age group, there
were "only 45.3 men for each 100 women."[8] Yet female-headed households
did not emerge in these places.

In some instances, the number of female-headed households may be attributed
to lack of gainful employment by men who often temporarily leave their families
for a considerable length of time in search of work elsewhere. In rural areas, particularly during the civil war, many men migrated to the cities, leaving the villages
almost exclusively to women and children. In other cases, which are common in

urban slums, men who are overburdened by financial obligations to the family simply abandon their homes. Women who head homes are thus also, often, wives abandoned by their husbands. In dislocated families without a male head, the burden of child rearing and general home management rests with the women.

As in many African cultures, age is highly respected in Angola. Family elders are regarded as custodians of wisdom, knowledge, and the values and customs of the society. The elders are therefore expected to tutor the younger members of the family in the intricacies of life. Considerable authority is placed in the hands of older male family members. In many ethnolinguistic groups among whom tradition still requires family rituals, the older men in the extended family are bestowed with the religious authority to do this. Different kinds of family rituals, such as ancestral spirit worship, are still common among rural people. In the cultures of many ethnolinguistic groups, such as the Ovimbundu, Bakongo, and Chokwe, sacrifices of food and drink to the spirits of departed family ancestors are required. They believe that if proper honor is accorded ancestral spirits through sacrifices, they will reciprocate by providing protection to the family and offer other blessings.

CHILDREN

Children are a precious and necessary part of the Angolan family. A household is not considered complete without children because childbearing is regarded as the primary reason for marriage. If a couple finds it difficult to produce children, the problem is often blamed on the woman, even in educated quarters. For some men, this is a license to take a second wife.

If the culture celebrates the male more than the female, as it is in most parts of Angola, boys are preferred to girls. A man is happier if his wife bears him sons rather than daughters. Multiple births of girls are sufficient grounds for a man to seek another wife who, hopefully, will give him sons. The age-old preference for male children has persisted even in cities and towns and among educated people.

Status and Roles

For children, status and roles are learned from family members, particularly parents. Girls' socialization is oriented toward making them subservient and teaching them the duties of a housewife, which they will perform in the future. In the household, girls help their mothers perform household chores such as cooking and washing and other tasks considered feminine. Boys, on the other hand, are socialized to play a more dominant role and are encouraged to help out in male-dominated vocations. Fathers often are a major influence on their male children.

Parents usually invest more in the education of boys than girls. It is not unusual to withdraw daughters from school to assist their mothers in household chores. Indeed, in Angola there has long been a great disparity between secondary school enrollments for boys and girls.

The socialization process for children continues through rites of passage, such as puberty rites for girls. In most of Angola today, particularly the urban areas, such rites are no longer practiced. Where they still exist, mostly in rural areas, they provide boys and girls an opportunity to learn the behaviors, norms, and values of their society. Among the Ovimbundu, girls' puberty rites include some instruction about sexual matters offered by elderly women.[9]

In general, a child is considered well brought up if he or she demonstrates good behavior. Respect for elders, for instance, is an important index of a good upbringing.

Social and Economic Conditions of Children

Angolan children face a dismal situation today. They are some of the worst treated children in the world. Severely abused and traumatized during the civil war, children endure pathetic social and economic conditions. In the past, the Angolan government did not give major consideration to promoting children's welfare and protecting their rights. Physical abuse of children is rampant; many lack adequate nutrition and face severe malnutrition. Child prostitution and trafficking in children for the purpose of sexual exploitation also have risen in postwar Angola.

In 2005, three years after the end of the Angolan civil war, the United Nations (UN) alerted the world to the severe children's malnutrition crisis in the country, especially in rural places. A World Food Programme (WFP) report indicated that about half of the children in Angola face severe malnourishment, which has resulted in stunted growth and contraction of preventable diseases such as tuberculosis.[10]

In many ways, Angola's children bore the disproportionate brunt of the civil war. Children, sometimes as young as 10 years old, were kidnapped and forcibly recruited into armed forces as combatants, especially by the National Union for the Total Independence of Angola (União Nacional para a Independência Total de Angola, UNITA). Children were injured and killed in battle and, more often than adults, were victims of land-mine explosions. They witnessed large-scale killings and were themselves forced to kill. Girls were used as sex slaves and endured various forms of sexual exploitation. This was rampant with UNITA, and underage girls served as concubines to commanders or forced into marriage with them.

In the postwar period, Angola faced the difficult problems of demobilizing child soldiers and reintegrating them into society. Governmental programs

Young children in happy disposition. However, many Angolan children traumatized by the long civil war still face an uncertain future. Courtesy of Armando J. Rodriguez, Jr.

and policies in areas such as education, health, nutrition, and food assistance were put in place and complemented by community, humanitarian, and religious initiatives. International nongovernmental organizations and UN agencies such as WFP, Save the Children, and the United Nations Children's Fund (UNICEF) also have been active in Angola in the area of child enrichment. Despite all these measures, safeguarding the welfare of Angola's children is still a major problem. According to reports, in 2005, more than 2 million children still suffered from emotional and physical deprivation.[11]

One of the most serious problems facing postwar Angola is the prevalence of street children. More than 100,000 children lost parents and family members during the war, and many of them have taken to the streets. Separated from parents, without any skills or formal education, and severely traumatized by the protracted conflict, these children roam the streets of major Angolan cities eking out a livelihood by doing odd jobs, begging, eating from trash cans, or otherwise engaging in petty crime.[12]

Prostitution involving underage girls also has become rampant in Luanda and other urban centers. Although the Angolan constitution makes prostitution illegal and child prostitution, in particular, a crime prohibited by a criminal statue, the laws have not been stringently enforced. Hundreds of young girls, the *catorzinhas* (literally, 14-year-olds), earn livings as prostitutes in Luanda and other cities. Trafficking of girls to neighboring states such as Namibia for prostitution also has been reported.[13]

Today, many Angolan children still face a bleak future. The National Children Institute (INAC), established by the government to improve the conditions of children, has been hampered by a lack of tools in its implementation of programs to aid children.

WOMEN AND SOCIETY

Women have always played diverse but important roles in modern Angola. Women's roles have remained the same in some respects, yet they have changed over time in other respects as a result of improved conditions in society. Women still play the primary role of housekeeper, fetch firewood for cooking, and sell wares in the market. Yet women have become writers, painters, musicians, and high officials of state. Mobilized effectively by the MPLA, the liberation war provided women a great opportunity to begin their own journey of self-determination.

Since independence, the conditions of women have improved significantly compared to what they were under colonialism. A number of women, though few, have occupied top-ranking positions within the government and the civil service, and many more have played important roles in politics, business, the military, and the professions. The reality of modern Angola, however, is that women are still largely relegated to a subservient position. Even though the constitution and other legal provisions ostensibly guarantee gender equality and women's rights, Angolan women generally continue to suffer discrimination and inequality in practically all areas of life.

The status of women in the society is undermined by two major factors. The first is the considerably lower educational standard of women compared to men. For decades, less attention was devoted to girls' education, and this is reflected today in a disproportionately lower literacy level for women than for men. Second, culture and social values still dictate a subordinate position for women. This traditional belief, which is not restricted to rural areas but occurs in urban centers as well, has stunted gender parity.

Given their general subservient status, women of Angola are susceptible to spousal abuse and domestic violence at home. Outside the home in the workplace, they suffer sexual harassment and discrimination. Reports of violence against women in the form of homicide have been made. In many instances in the past, existing legal provisions could not prevent mistreatment of women due to limited resources for prosecution.

Efforts to bridge gender disparity and guarantee women's rights, however, are alive in Angola through the government and women's organizations.

Since the end of the civil war, the laws have been more effectively enforced in punishing crimes against women, such as rape and assault. The Ministry of Women and Family Affairs has the responsibility of dealing with issues related to women's rights. Women's organizations also have been active.

The Organization of Angolan Women (Organização da Mulher Angolana, OMA), formed in 1962 and affiliated with the MPLA, is the largest women's organization in the country. Since its foundation, the OMA has played a prominent role in raising Angolan women's consciousness about their rights under the law. The organization has been instrumental in the achievement of a greater level of political and social participation by women.[14]

Women's high susceptibility to HIV infection deserves some mention. The AIDS pandemic has been particularly devastating in Angola, but women are more vulnerable to infection than men. First, this is because women are the primary caregivers to people living with HIV/AIDS. This raises their susceptibility to infection. Second, in a patriarchal, male-dominated society in which the culture expects women to be submissive to their husbands, they cannot resist sexual advances from husbands who practice risky sexual behaviors.[15]

In the informal sector, which is a significant portion of the urban economy, women have played an important role. Retail is a female-dominated arena of the Angolan economy, and women's entrepreneurial activities include selling a variety of retail merchandise and foodstuffs. Despite the importance of the informal sector, the government has largely ignored it, and few laws protect market women and those involved in petty commercial activities from the vagaries of the economy, such as hyperinflation. Women in the informal sector lack, among other things, access to training programs to enhance their productivity, capital in the form of microloans for expansion, and an effective lobby group. Invariably, petty entrepreneurs in Angola, mostly women and largely illiterate, constitute the most susceptible sector of the labor market.

NOTES

1. International Lesbian and Gay Association, *World Legal Survey.*
2. Owomoyela, "African Literature."
3. See "Family Minister Condemns Premature Marriage."
4. Cited in Tvedten, *Angola,* 105. See details of the study in Curtis, *Water and Women's Work.*
5. Tvedten, *Angola,* 116.
6. Cited in Santos, *Beyond Inequalities,* 34.
7. See for instance, Colaço, *A situacao da mulher em Angola;* Hurlich, *Angola;* and Tvedten, *Angola,* 105.
8. Tvedten, *Angola,* 117.

9. See Hambly, *The Ovimbundu of Angola.*

10. See Neighbour, "Half of Angola's Children Malnourished." For a full report, see World Food Program/Vulnerability Analysis and Mapping, *Food Security and Livelihood Survey.*

11. UN Office for the Coordination of Humanitarian Affairs, "Angola: Children Ravaged by War," *Integrated Regional Information Networks (IRIN)*, February 1, 2005, http://www.irinnews.org/report.asp?ReportID=43401.

12. For a report on street children in Angola, see "Angola: The Forgotten Victims," 1.

13. The Bureau of Democracy, Human Rights, and Labor, "Country Reports on Human Rights Practices 2002," reports child trafficking and child prostitution.

14. For more details on the OMA, see dos Santos, *Beyond Inequalities;* and Organização da Mulher Angola, *Liberation in Southern Africa.*

15. For more on this subject, see Castelo, Gaspan, and Félix, "A Cultural Approach to HIV/AIDS Prevention and Care"; and dos Santos, *Beyond Inequalities.*

7

Social Customs and Lifestyle

SOCIAL CUSTOMS OF the Angolan people are rooted in their culture and traditions as well as their historical experiences from precolonial times to the present. Some traditional customs are no longer practiced in contemporary Angola, whereas others are performed infrequently and are restricted to rural populations. Yet many traditional social customs still constitute an important component of social life. Although customs differ from one ethnolinguistic group to another, it is only in the details. For instance, irrespective of the manner in which each group performs ceremonies and rites, these customs serve the same utilitarian purpose in all Angolan cultures of furthering societal well-being and harmony and individual fortunes and progress. Angolans share the fundamental belief that performance of ceremonies and rituals invite and confer on communities, families, and individuals the favorable disposition of the spirit world.

Angola is a dynamic society that continues to evolve and transform itself in response to social change and economic conditions. For instance, the infusions of Western values into the Angolan culture have greatly impacted old ways and traditions in such a manner that some customs have been modified or transformed.

Lifestyle draws from traditional customs, but it also reflects socioeconomic changes brought about by increased Westernization and other variables such as the long and devastating civil war. Urbanized and educated Angolans exhibit patterns of social behavior that have been greatly influenced by Western culture. Also, the civil war experience bears some relations to lifestyle, especially in areas devastated by the long conflict. Although lifestyle may differ from one socioeconomic situation to another, the people of Angola, to a large extent, share common patterns of social behavior.

SOCIAL RELATIONS

Angolans are not culturally individualistic, whether they are urban or rural dwellers, whether they are traditional or modern in outlook. Communal life and social interaction are important and expressed in diverse ways. Despite the untold devastation brought to the society by the brutal civil war, the constraints of a collapsed economy, and degraded life conditions, Angolans remain generally a warm, friendly, and hospitable people.

Traditional Society

In the past and in contemporary societies that are predominantly traditional, festivals, ceremonies, and rituals offer opportunities for social relations. These are performed within extended families, lineages, villages, and other subgroups, and they provide an avenue by which people come together to interact, felicitate, and celebrate.

Because the extended family is an important unit of social relations, strong kinship ties enhance social interactions. Age is very important in individual behavior and interpersonal relationships within the family. It is customary for younger people to relate to their elders in a respectful manner because age is revered. For instance, children not only have a duty to greet adults, they also must do so in a way that shows respect for age. It would be inappropriate for someone to greet a person as old as his parents with *"Olá"* (Hi) and without a bow. Greetings are, indeed, valued, and there are forms of greetings for almost every task and every occasion.

Elders relate to younger people in a manner that befits their status as custodians of wisdom. Normally, they dispense instructions, particularly relating to traditional values and societal norms, which the young accept without question. This is the pattern of social relations through which the culture is transmitted from one generation to the next.

Social groups in the past also served as agents of interpersonal relations. Age-group associations were effective tools of relationships among people of the same age group. Members of age-group associations could assist a fellow member in tasks such as completing a house. Age-group associations also help build group identity and provide forums, through meetings and get-togethers, for the development of interpersonal relationships.

Modern Society

Social relations follow various avenues in modern Angola. Interaction in a personal way is always valued when it comes to discussion of important issues such as family matters and business transactions. Even when access to technological devices such as the telephone and e-mail are available, one-on-one discussion of important matters is still preferred.

Communal relationship is still strong, even in the cities and towns where urban life patterns tend to promote individualism. Angolans love to attend social functions and events where they socialize, celebrate, and meet people. Partying is very popular, and amid economic hardship some people still throw lavish parties that often feature music and dance as well as different foods and drinks, including alcoholic beverages. Although some parties may require a formal invitation, usually most parties do not, and no one is turned away. Nightlife activities also offer opportunities for social gatherings and the building of social relations.

Greeting is still valued in social behavior in the modern society, although Western influence has diminished its traditional importance. In urban areas, greeting is more informal. Although respect is still accorded elders, it is sufficient for people, especially peers, to greet one another in more informal ways. Generally, people show courtesy with handshakes and hugs that may be accompanied by friendly back slaps. Some who are more Westernized add kissing on the check while greeting a person of the opposite sex. For most people, the verbalization of everyday greetings such as "Good morning," "How do you do," and other forms is done in the local languages. More formal settings, on the other hand, might call for greetings in Portuguese.

CEREMONIES

Ceremonies are important both in the traditional and in the modern culture of the Angolan people. The most common ceremonies are those pertaining to life. Childbirth and a naming ceremony herald the arrival of a baby into this world, initiation inducts adolescents into adulthood, marriage confers procreation and parentage rights, and rites of transition prepare the dead for the afterlife. It is important to look more closely at these traditional customs.

Childbirth, Names, and the Naming Ceremony

As in other places, in Angola childbirth is an occasion for joy for the family. It is a fulfillment of marriage because tradition regards a family without children as unfulfilled.

In traditional societies, pregnant women are cared for and nursed in the home throughout their pregnancy by older women. This situation prevails mainly in rural areas, and this means that many rural women do not enjoy modern medical prenatal monitoring and counseling regarding issues such as hygiene, nutrition, and family planning. Delivery is also often done at home and handled by traditional birth attendants who are more often than not untrained in the medical procedure. Lack of proper prenatal care and nonaccess to hospital delivery and postnatal care combine to make Angola a country with one of the high rates of mortality among pregnant women in the world.

One of the reasons for the prevalence of prenatal home care and delivery among rural women is difficulties in gaining access to modern medical facilities. Hospitals and even clinics are often not available within reasonable distances so that a pregnant woman must travel far to find one. In many places, travel to hospitals is hazardous because of impassable roads or roads laden with land mines. Generally, however, in Angola health care is in crisis because hospitals lack basic necessities like drugs, equipment, and an adequate number of medical personnel, especially doctors.

With assistance from international nongovernmental organizations, Angola has made improvements in the health-care sector, particularly since the civil war ended. Because many rural women have no other choice but to rely on birth attendants, training programs have been organized for them as a way to reduce maternal and infant mortality rates. One such training program was developed by the International Medical Corps (IMC) for prenatal care, delivery, and postnatal care.[1]

A naming ceremony is the formal welcoming of a newborn into the world. The timing of the ceremony and paraphernalia vary from place to place. Essentially, in traditional societies, the ceremony involves the parents of the child and family members and is directed by an elder in the family who confers on the child the names that the father has provided. Prayers for the child and its family are also offered in the name of the ancestors. In more educated circles, the child's names may be a joint decision of both parents. In Christian homes, a clergyman, rather than an elderly family member, is given charge of the ceremony, and it is conducted with Bible readings and prayers. Baptism in the church often accompanies a Christian naming ceremony.

As in many African cultures, traditional names in Angola are given based on some consideration, such as circumstances of the birth of a child or some family conditions. Names thus reflect a person's history and define his personality and identity. It is also common practice among many ethnolinguistic groups to name children after ancestors, following the belief that the ancestor will protect a person who bears his name.

A change in a person's circumstances may require a name change. For instance, among some ethnolinguistic groups, boys and girls often change their names after initiation to signify their transition to adulthood. During the liberation war, name changing was popular, and many Popular Movement for the Liberation of Angola (Movimento Popular de Libertação de Angola, MPLA) fighters changed their names.[2] The reason for adopting war names was described by a former MPLA guerrilla in 1996:

We changed our names. ... [Agostinho] Neto explained to us: "If in the bush you keep on using the name with which they used to call you at home, the Portuguese will kill all your relatives. They will say: 'That guy we have been looking for is in the bush.' If they find your parents, your father and your mother, they will kill them both. You must use other names that are not known by the Portuguese and not recorded in their books." In the beginning I called myself Cisukuti (Boomslang). After Cisukuti, my name became Kandungu (Chili Pepper). And from Kandungu I changed to Konkili (Concrete), and I am still called thus by now.[3]

During the colonial period, Angolan Christian converts were required by the church missions to change their names before they could be baptized. Today, it is fashionable for many people, especially the educated class, to give their children Portuguese names rather than African names.

Initiation Ceremonies

Traditional Angolan society has different initiation rites, and they are an important expression of social customs. Although the importance of these rites is greatly diminished in contemporary times and their practice restricted to some rural communities, they still represent a vital and sacred feature of the culture of many ethnolinguistic groups.

One of the most popular social customs in traditional society is the rite of puberty (iniciação da puberdade) in which boys and girls are initiated into adulthood when they become of age. This custom is primarily intended to prepare young people for their respective social roles as adult men and women. The initiation rites are elaborate, lasting several weeks, even months in some places, and ending with days of celebration by the entire community.

Male initiation rites are conducted in the woods, where the boys, who are often around the age of 15, are camped for months. Among other things, during this period they undergo training in the rituals and traditions of the community. Initiation rites also often include instructions on sexual matters in order to groom the boys for their impending marital role and other duties that adulthood entrusts to them. Most initiation rites require the boys to be subjected to a test of courage and fortitude. Thus, their sojourn in the camp includes a trial of survival in which they stay alone in the forest for a specific period of time. Among many ethnolinguistic groups, a central feature of puberty rites is the male circumcision ritual called *mukanda* by the Lunda-Chokwe.

Masquerade dance is an important feature of boys' initiation rites. The use of masks is so central to the rites that among the Chokwe the initiates are taught the art of mask carving. A popular Chokwe puberty circumcision mask is the female mask of Mwana Pwo, which is worn by male dancers during the puberty rites. Also among the Chokwe, the *cikunza* masquerade is important in a puberty rite because it is believed to promote fertility. Initiation masks are popular among other groups such as the Yaka and are worn by initiation leaders during the ceremonies. Mask wearing is also considered a celebration of an adolescent's coming of age.

Female initiation rites (*wali*, among the Chokwe and related peoples) are conducted when a girl reaches the age when she can bear children. The girls are beautifully adorned with traditional makeup and hairdos, and their initiation ceremonies feature ritual dances. The initiation rituals prepare the girls for wifehood and motherhood through training under the direction of elderly women. Their training stresses a woman's sexual submission to her husband and focuses on the general issue of the traditional woman's role in society. In some Angolan communities, girls' puberty rites do not involve circumcision. It is an important part of rites among some other groups, however, most especially in southern Angola. The circumcision of girls is traditionally thought to ease childbirth.

For the young men, the completion of the *mukanda* rite signifies the attainment of adulthood. As men, they must now associate with other men, not with children and women, as was the case prior to the initiation rites. The initiated girl is also now considered a woman and is eligible for marriage. A time of community celebration follows the completion of the rites of passage. The length of the celebration, which features dancing and feasting, varies according to the community but usually lasts for several days. The welcome ceremonies for the newly initiated boys include the *makishi* masquerade dance.

Death and Funerary Rites

In Angola, just as childbirth calls for a ceremony to celebrate new life, death is also accompanied by funerary rites. Many Angolan communities expect proper funeral rites to be observed and certain rituals to be performed for a dead person. Funerary rites vary from one ethnolinguistic group to another, but the general elements of these rites include ritual mourning, ceremonial washing of the body, and the embracing and kissing of the body by family members.

It is a strongly held belief, even in contemporary Angola, that life continues after death but in spirit form. Therefore, failure to perform proper funerary rites denies the departed a perfect rest in peace or entry into the abode of the ancestors. The consequence of this is aimless wandering of the restless spirit of the dead, which is considered inimical to the welfare of the living.

The widely held belief that the neglect to perform funerary rites at the death of a person is ominous to the society is demonstrated in the attitude of many Angolans to the thousands who died during the civil war without the opportunity to be honored by proper burial rituals. Many people still grapple with the guilt of not according these victims of war a dignified burial. It is believed that their spirits are unhappy and thus cause bad things to happen in the community.

Alcinda Honwana has provided some case studies of the expression of this belief by Angolans.[4] During the war in 1992–94, thousands of people were killed in the town of Kuito, on the plateau of Bié in central Angola. No burial rituals were performed for the dead; the bodies could not be reached and identified because of land mines, and many remained on the plateau until 1997. To avoid afflictions in Kuito as a result of the perceived anger of the unsettled spirits of these dead people, many in the town called for government assistance in performing the proper burial rites for them in order to appease them. According to the traditional chief in Kuito:

The government must think of having collective ceremonies to bury the bones of those killed in the war…. Here in Kuito many people died and no ceremonies were performed to appease their souls. Their souls are wandering about and can afflict anyone.[5]

The strong belief in modern Angola in the performance of traditional funerary rites was also expressed in 2005 when many people died, particularly in the northern province of Uíge, from the deadly hemorrhagic fever related to Ebola caused by the Marburg virus. Health workers had a hard time convincing people to avoid contact with the bodies of the victims because of the highly contagious nature of the disease. Families insisted on performing the traditional ritual that required embracing and kissing the corpses.

Child participation in funeral proceedings is defined by the particular culture. In some communities, children are not allowed to take part in burial rites under the belief that they may be afflicted by the spirit of the dead person. In other communities, however, children play certain roles. For instance, in Kuito children are made to pass under the coffin of a dead parent during the funeral ceremony. The same ritual is also practiced in Malange, and its purpose is to prevent the child from being afflicted by the spirit of the dead person. As is practiced in Malange, children are expected to cut their hair to show mourning and respect for the departed relative.[6]

Ancestral Worship and Veneration

Ancestral worship, which includes veneration, is central to the culture of most Angolan ethnolinguistic groups. Ancestral worship involves ritual ceremonies conducted by families or entire communities to appease and court the good favor of ancestors. Ancestors are believed to be alive in spirit with the power to protect the community, families, and individuals that they left behind. Their good disposition requires ceremonial rituals that are preformed usually at regular periods. Sometimes, a prevailing condition, such as prolonged lack of rain or outbreak of disease, may call for ancestral worship.

Ancestral worship may be conducted by special initiates who carry out all the rituals. This is true mostly of family units in which the necessary sacrifices to the family ancestor are carried out by a designated elder. On the other hand, ancestral worship may involve the entire community when it is in veneration of the groups' ancestor. In this instance, the ritual becomes a village festival featuring feasting, dancing, and general celebration. Sacrifices to the ancestors include food and drink, but animals such as goats, oxen, and chickens are also sometimes slaughtered and offered as sacrifice.

Healing Ceremonies

Healing ceremonies are popular, especially in traditional Angolan societies where they are aimed at curing every imaginable affliction or disease, from simple ailments such as fever, stomachache, and bad dreams to more severe conditions, including female sterility and mental disorder. Despite modern medicine and hospitals, many Angolans, particularly in rural areas, still patronize traditional healers *(kimbanda)* who perform these ceremonies.

Traditional healing ceremonies generally focus on symbolic cleansing and purification rituals. Illnesses or afflictions are believed to involve spirits *(mahamba,* among the Lwena), so the aim of a healing ceremony is to exorcise the bad spirit from the victim. Treatment regimens administered by the traditional healer include serving the patient herbal concoctions usually made with boiled leaves, roots, and other condiments. The patient must either drink, inhale, or take a steam bath with the remedy over a period of time as instructed by the *kimbanda.* The healing ritual is not complete without symbolic activation of the medicine in the form of communion with the spirit world through incantations by the traditional healer. Other rituals might be performed to purify the patient and sever any lingering link he might still have with the bad spirit.

Healing rituals may be performed in the open or in secret, depending on the type of sickness or the tradition of the community. When it is an open ritual, family and community members are allowed to attend. In fact, the rituals may require active community participation for proper cleansing.

In contemporary Angola, many people, particularly in rural communities, still trust and patronize traditional healers. This was seen in the recourse to traditional medicine during the outbreak of the Marburg virus. Traditional healing has particularly gained prominence in Angola in the post–civil war period because of the need to heal thousands of former child soldiers who had willingly or otherwise committed atrocities during the war. For those children, the culture required cleansing and purification rituals to release them from haunting and avenging spirits of the people they had killed. Rather than seeking modern therapeutic treatment, such children are referred to traditional healers. Green and Honwana have recorded typical healing rituals performed for former child combatants. According to a case in Uíge:

When the child or young man returns home, he is made to wait on the outskirts of the village. The oldest woman from the village throws maize flour at the boy and anoints his entire body with a chicken. He is only able to enter the village after this ritual is complete. After the ritual, he is allowed to greet his family in the village. Once the greeting is over, he must kill a chicken, which is subsequently cooked and served to the family. For the first eight days after the homecoming, he is not allowed to sleep in his own bed, only on a rush mat on the floor. During this time, he is taken to the river and water is poured on his head and he is given manioc to eat. As he leaves the site of the ritual, he must not look behind him.[7]

Some traditional healers have clinics at which prolonged healing rituals are performed for those admitted for sicknesses like madness, which is believed to have been caused by evil spirits. Abuses and other medical irregularities have been reported in many of these healing homes, however. For instance, patients are usually housed in poor living quarters, and those who try to incorporate modern medical practice into their trade have reused syringes on multiple patients and sometimes dispense drugs wrongfully. Some who cater to patients with mental disorders often chained them to the floor for a long period of time if they are considered dangerous.

In competition with traditional healers and modern medical practitioners are church leaders who have gone into the healing business. This is true of many traditional Kimbanguist and even some mainstream Pentecostal churches. These churches often perform exorcisms on people suspected of possession by evil spirits *(kindoki)* or attacked by witchcraft. Church healing ceremonies, often led by pastors, prophets, or prophetesses, are often accompanied by fervent prayer sessions and the use of holy water and lighted candles to drive out the evil spirit from the possessed.

Modern Religious Ceremonies

Angola is a country with a large Christian population; therefore, modern religious ceremonies follow rituals of the Christian faiths. Christmas and Easter are the most popular Christian feasts in Angola, and they are celebrated as public holidays.

During Christmas season, churches and schools, particularly parochial ones, organize special events like community outreach, services of carols, and plays. In reality, Christmas is celebrated by nearly everyone, irrespective of creed. More than its religious significance, the Christmas season is always a time for people to socialize and enjoy themselves. Throughout the season, parties are held everywhere, organized by individuals, families, and social groups to bring friends and relatives together to socialize. The biggest parties of the season, often lasting all night, are reserved for Christmas Eve.

In Angola, Christmas Day is a designated family day, and an emphasis is placed on family get-togethers and celebrations. Family members living in other places, even far away from home, often return for the reunions. Because food is important for the celebration of the season, sumptuous Christmas feasts are prepared in many households. Common Christmas dishes include rice, potatoes, turkey, meat, fish, and vegetables to go along with delicacies such as cakes and wine. Gifts may also be exchanged among family members.

Of course, one of the events marking Christmas is church attendance on December 25. Everyone is expected to be well and colorfully dressed for church. In the evening, people go about visiting friends, acquaintances, and neighbors, presenting gifts if they can afford to do so.

Christmas is not a commercial enterprise in Angola as in many Western countries. The exchange of gifts is not overtly emphasized, particularly expensive ones. Giving gifts is often done by wealthier families. In urban places, some houses may be decorated with Christmas trees, flowers, fruits, and lights.

The Easter season is also celebrated in Angola each spring, although in a more religious and sober manner that lacks the pomp and fanfare of Christmas. The events marking the season usually begin on Palm Sunday when the faithful commemorate the triumphant entry of Jesus Christ into Jerusalem. Good Friday is a public holiday, and although church services are not usually held, many devout Christians spend time in religious devotions such as fasting and praying. Some churches organize street processions and plays in commemoration of the suffering that Jesus Christ endured at the Crucifixion. Easter Sunday is celebrated with a mass, and most churches are packed full. Easter Monday is also a public holiday; many people go on picnics or otherwise enjoy themselves in some leisure activity.

HOLIDAYS

Public holidays in Angola are generally of two types: secular and religious. Secular holidays can be further subdivided into two categories. One category includes national holidays that are observed or celebrated nationwide in both the public and the private sectors.

Perhaps, the most important national holiday is Independence Day, celebrated on November 11 every year in commemoration of independence from Portugal after a long war of national liberation. The first Independence Day was celebrated in 1976. In 2005, the 30th anniversary was elaborately commemorated, the first time in relative peace and economic and political progress since independence. Thousands of Angolans, optimistic about the future of their country, thronged the Estádio da Cidadela (Cidadela Stadium) in Luanda to witness the events marking the anniversary, which included a speech by President Eduardo dos Santos. The occasion also brought to Luanda several dignitaries and foreign heads of state.

Following is a complete list of national public holidays:

January 1: New Year's Day.

February 4: Liberation Day. This is the National Armed Struggle Day established in commemoration of the beginning of the war of liberation against Portuguese colonialism.

March 8: International Women's Day.

April 4: Peace and National Reconciliation Day.

May 1: Labor (Workers') Day.

May 25: Africa Freedom Day.

June 1: International Children's Day.

September 17: National Hero's Day. This is held to commemorate the anniversary of the birthday of Angola's first postindependence president, Agostinho Neto.

November 2: All Souls' Day.

November 11: Independence Day.

December 10: MPLA Foundation Day. This is in the celebration of the anniversary of the foundation of the ruling party, the MPLA-Labor Party.

The second category of secular holidays includes those that are unofficial but widely celebrated. They include the following:

March 27: Victory Day

April 14: Youth Day

August 1: Armed Forces' Day

December 1: Pioneers' Day

Religious holidays in Angola are solely those in commemoration of Christian festivals. These holidays are Good Friday and Easter Monday, variably held in March or April, and Christmas Day on December 25. No holidays commemorate traditional religious festivals of other religions like Islam. The grant of Christian holidays is reflective of the strong Christian, particularly Roman Catholic, influence in Angola.

CHANGE IN SOCIAL CUSTOMS AND LIFESTYLE

Culture is not static; rather, it is dynamic. Although some aspects of Angolan culture die hard, others have seen significant transformations.

In general, Angolan society has undergone changes in all areas of human endeavor: political, social, economic, and cultural.

Transformations in cultural practices are not evenly distributed in Angola. Cultural differences exist between the rural and the urban person, between the educated and the illiterate, between a devout Christian and a practitioner of traditional religion, and between people of different socioeconomic classes. All Angolans have faced the forces of change, but generally, they have demonstrated remarkable ability to adapt to changes.

Western Impact on Customs and Lifestyle

The most important agent of social change in Angola, as in most African states, is Western culture. The Portuguese colonial system condemned and undercut indigenous culture. It generally introduced new political, social, and economic institutions to replace traditional ones. It also elevated Western values above indigenous values. Western education, particularly promoted by Christian missions, helped impose foreign values.

During the colonial period, traditional power structures were severely weakened. Traditional chieftains and authority institutions were relegated and subordinated to the colonial authority. A modern judiciary based on the Portuguese legal system was developed to resolve conflicts between families, neighbors, and others, rather than head chiefs. A new uniformed police force had the responsibility to keep law and maintain order, and an organized army became the custodian of state security.

The postindependence state that emerged continued with the existing system of government and did not return traditional authority to its precolonial dispensation. Western education and the influence of Christianity further entrenched foreign cultural values. Urbanized, educated Christian and Westernized Angolans, few at first, increasingly abandoned traditional practices. Social change in Angola has thus meant the erosion of many traditional practices such as initiation ceremonies, or it has led to the modification of others such as marriage ceremonies infused with Western culture. Some ceremonies are entirely Western imports, such as Christmas and Easter.

In modern Angola, education has come to be seen—and quite correctly—as a means of acquiring high social status. Social habits of the growing educated class of the urban areas are not usually in line with tradition. With easier access to information projected by the media, both local and foreign, and limited Internet and cell phone access, many educated Angolans are provided with the opportunity to relate to the outside world and acquire foreign values. For example, at least in the major towns and cities, Western popular music is widely known, many people dress in Western-style clothing, and many speak Portuguese.

Needless to say, education is also the key to gainful employment. Good jobs open the door to new patterns of consumption. As people move up the economic ladder, they develop tastes for Western products and lifestyle. Consequently, traditional culture recedes. Although age is still important as a source of respect, wealth and education now go a long way to define a person's social status in society. Women increasingly acquire education and move into the professional workplace, thus altering the traditional women's role.

New agents of social interaction also have developed in modern Angola. Professional associations, social clubs, and church-based groups have replaced age-group associations in facilitating social interaction. For example, professional bodies such the Associação de journalists das mulheres de Angola (Association of Women Journalists of Angola, AMUJA) and the Associação Angolan Dos Médicos (Angolan Physicians Association, AMEA) not only promote their members' professional interests but also serve their social interests by providing an avenue for social interaction among members.

Urban Survival

Rapid urbanization in Angola has not been accompanied by development of necessary infrastructure. For instance, during the war the population of Luanda swelled but without building adequate infrastructure to serve the population explosion. Today, major Angolan cities lack adequate supplies of treated water, efficient transportation systems, reliable power supplies, and working sanitation systems. The lack of basic amenities has affected lifestyle.

In Angola, the vast majority of the people is impoverished and lives a low-quality life. Poverty and family dislocation have driven many children to lives on the street where they eek out a living from odd jobs and petty crime. In Luanda, for instance, school-age boys on the streets are often involved in mugging, pick pocketing, purse snatching, auto break-ins, and home invasions. Their female counterparts usually end up living as prostitutes. High unemployment has driven other older people into a life of crime. Those gainfully employed may also be engaged in white-collar crime. Corruption is rampant at every level of society. For instance, police and government officials take bribes.

In the midst of glaring poverty among the majority, the rich still live ostentatious lifestyles. They display their wealth through expensive clothing, flashy cars, big modern houses in affluent neighborhoods, and lavish parties. Their lifestyle is radically different, for example, from that of people living in Luanda's *musséques,* many of whom are engaged in menial jobs, if they are employed at all. The urban lifestyle is also quite different from the rural one. Urban centers provide work for many people in the production and service sectors, even if the unemployment rate is still high. People who work in the professions as journalists, lawyers, doctors, accountants, teachers, and the like earn good incomes and thus are able to move up the social ladder. In the villages, on the other hand, many people are involved in peasant agricultural work, tilling the ground with archaic farm tools. The kinds of work people are engaged in greatly reflect their lifestyles and attitudes to life. For instance, a professor at Agostinho Neto University in Luanda with an appreciably high standard of living may want to limit his family to two or three children. His counterpart in some village, a farmer barely living above the poverty level, on the other hand may favor a family of six children.

Lifestyle and the AIDS Crisis

The AIDS pandemic that has hit Angola hard has also significantly affected lifestyle. The first AIDS cases were said to have been diagnosed in 1985. Since then, a large number of Angolans have been infected with the deadly virus. In the past in traditional societies, the culture placed emphasis on sexual restraint. The abuse of the Western concept of sexuality that gives latitude to sexual behavior has allowed risky sexual behavior in the form of multiple sexual partners, especially among young people, the group most vulnerable to HIV infection.

AIDS is prevalent in the major cities such as Luanda. In the country, the age range of those mostly affected is 30 to 40 years. The high-risk groups include sex workers, truck drivers, soldiers, prisoners, and sailors, and the main path of HIV transmission is through heterosexual sex.

In the past, Angolans, especially the youth who are mostly at risk of contracting HIV, were ill informed about the disease and were poorly equipped to fight it. Slowly, Angolans are becoming better informed and educated about the disease and thus are forced to modify their sexual lifestyles. In addition to government efforts through the health ministry, many agencies are involved in the nationwide AIDS awareness and prevention program. AIDS education is aimed at providing information and eliminating ignorance about the disease.

NOTES

1. For details, see Schaider, Ngonyani, Tomlin, Rydman, and Roberts, "International Maternal Mortality Reduction."

2. For a discussion of this, see Brinkman, "Language, Names, and War."

3. Ibid., 143.

4. See Honwana, "Non-Western Concepts of Mental Health."

5. Cited in ibid.

6. The analysis here is based on Honwana, "*Okusiakala ondalo yokalye.*"

7. Green and Honwana, "Indigenous Healing of War-Affected Children in Africa."

8

Music and Dance

It is said that only my songs have the power to make both President dos Santos and UNITA's leader, Jonas Savimbi, dance together.[1]
——Waldemar Bastos, Angolan musician

The Civil War started. ... The music industry just stopped. No one had cash. No one had time. No studios. No producers. Musicians emigrated to other countries. The music did not stop but there was very little recording.[2]
——Mario Futado, Banda Maravilha's drummer

AN EXPOSITION ON the culture and customs of the people of Angolan would be incomplete without a discussion of the music and the dance forms of the people. Indeed, the country has an incredibly rich cultural tradition in the areas of music and dance. Practically all ethnolinguistic groups relish music and dance, and these historically have played an important role in their cultural development.

In precolonial times, music and dance constituted an integral part of everyday life, and practically every social event, including ceremonies, rituals, festivals, and carnivals, had a component of music and dance. In modern times, music continues to be an important part of life and a strong vehicle of social relations. Wherever there is music, Angolans do not loose the opportunity to dance. Music and dance occur in every social situation, in joyous occasions such as childbirth celebrations and marriage ceremonies or in grieving occasions such as funerals, especially of elderly persons.

Modern Angolan music has been influenced by the music tradition of other cultures, most notably Brazil and Cuba. The music is also greatly influenced by Portugal; Portuguese is the language of musical expression for many musicians. Elements of Angolan traditional music, in turn, are present in the music of other lands. Angola's *semba* is the parent of Brazil's samba. African American jazz rhythms borrow, in part, from Angolan music.

DEVELOPMENT OF ANGOLAN MUSIC

Traditional Music

Traditional music constitutes a vital aspect of the social and religious experience in Angola. Songs are an integral part of social functions such as child namings, marriage ceremonies, installations of a chiefs, funeral rites, and village festivals. For such occasions, special songs are rendered and accompanied by prescribed instruments. At appropriate situations, folk songs and other secular songs perform the social function of entertaining, instructing, and educating.

Music is also present in every religious event and ritual, such as initiation ceremonies. The main events of boys' initiation into adulthood, the *mukanda* for instance, are accompanied by music and masquerade dancing *(makishi)*. Ritual songs provide the avenue for communicating with ancestral spirits or higher deities. The chanting of ritual songs, apart from sacrifices, is a form of ancestral worship necessary to cleanse the land of evil and invite the goodwill of the ever-watching ancestors.

Traditional musicians used to play a prominent role in the social life of communities. They played the drums and other traditional instruments at official ceremonies and social occasions. Court musicians, for instance, the players of royal flutes among the Ovimbundu, also performed.

Traditional forms of music have been significantly undercut by Euro-Christian Western culture and urbanization. This change dates to the colonial period when Christian missionaries and the colonial powers frowned on most aspects of Angolan traditional culture, which were perceived as heathen, including the music. Indeed, the rendering of traditional songs and playing of musical instruments was regarded as contemptuous by the colonial authority. Except in some rural communities, many traditional practices that require traditional songs have largely disappeared from the Angolan contemporary reality. Nevertheless, many Angolan musicians and bands used folk music as a cultural weapon of resistance against the colonial authority in the late colonial period.

Modern Music and Musicians

Modern Angolan music emerged in the 1940s when a Luanda-based musical group of nine artists known as Ngola Ritmos was created and led by Liceu

Vieira Dias. Dias, who could be described as the father of modern Angolan popular music, is a multitalented musician adept on the acoustic guitar and conga drums. His musical group, Ngola Ritmos, achieved widespread popularity in Angola in the late colonial era of the 1950s with its rhythmic and melodious dance music.

Ngola Ritmos played traditional and contemporary rhythms with modern instruments like electric guitar in urban areas. Yet the band was also political, making effective use of anticolonial lyrics in the vernacular, particularly Kimbundu, in support of the independence movement. The band members were militant nationalists; Dias himself was a founding member of the Popular Movement for the Liberation of Angola (Movimento Popular de Libertação de Angola, MPLA). As a result of Ngola Ritmos's politically motivated urban popular music, the Portuguese colonial authority considered the group a threat to its power and had Dias arrested in 1959. Arrest and detention of Angolan radical artists, including musicians suspected by the colonial authority of sympathy toward the nationalist cause, were quite common in the decades preceding independence.

Ngola Ritmos continued to be active after the detention of Dias. Its political message of nationalism clothed in authentic Angolan rhythm rendered in local languages resonated with the people. The group achieved a number of hit songs, such as "Django Ué," but the colonial authority sought to stifle its music, which it regarded as subversive. To some extent, colonial repression retarded the flowering of modern music in Angola, but the Portuguese were unable to halt the country's musical outburst. Faced with resentment from the population in the early 1960s, the colonial authority was forced to relax its stranglehold on Angolan popular culture and artistic expression.

One of the legacies of Ngola Ritmos was its lead in the development of Angola's nationalist music during the early preindependence period, which played an important role in the anticolonial struggle that eventually won independence for Angola in 1975. The band also influenced the emergence of new musical groups and musicians. In the 1960s and 1970s, electric-guitar pop bands such as Os Kiezos, Orquestra os Jovens do Prenda, Oscar Neves, and Os Bongos became prominent on the Angolan music scene. Supported by the burgeoning recording industry in Angola, these bands produced hits that were influenced by Brazilian and Caribbean music, local rhythms of *semba* and *rebita,* and Congolese rumba. Some 1960s hits included Os Kiezos's "Muxima" and "Princeza Rita," Os Jovens Do Prenda's "Lamento De Mae," Os Bongos's "Kazukuta," and Oscar Neves's "Tia Sessa and Mundanda."

Shaped by the anticolonial movement, however, much Angolan music in the immediate postindependence era was predictably political and controversial. Like Angolan literature, music focused on the social degradation and the chaotic life brought about by the escalating postindependence civil war. The preponderance of implicit political content in Angola's music constrained and discouraged thematic and stylistic innovations. Further, the civil war, which was generally destructive of Angola's cultural infrastructure, wiped out the nation's recording industry, and artists were forced to seek production opportunities abroad.

Despite the hard times of popular culture brought about by the civil war, some of the bands that had evolved in the 1960s managed to stay in existence in some form in the early 1970s, mainly by playing live in the major cities. By the late 1980s and early 1990s, however, Angolan music had begun to be infused with new talent and greater creativity. Even though the war was ongoing, new varieties of music developed, including rock and rap. Despite prevailing deplorable wartime social and economic conditions and livelihood, Angola's musicians began to explore new themes in their lyrics that were suggestive of romance, sex, love, and other mundane subjects. Some adapted traditional culture by infusing folklore into their art. Generally, the musicians sang in both Portuguese and indigenous languages.

Musicians

Modern Angola has produced a number of highly acclaimed musicians, some of whom are known internationally. One of the best-known Angolan musicians with a reputation beyond the country's borders is the Afro-pop musician Jose Adelino Barceló de Carvalho, who is more popularly known in the world of music as Bonga (or Bonga Kuenda). A onetime athlete and professional soccer star, Bonga is a veteran of Angolan music and has many hits to show for it. In the early 1960s he founded a musical group, Kissueia (meaning "the misery of the poor areas" in Kimbundu), whose music offered a biting social critique of Angola under colonial rule. A product of the *musseques* of Luanda, Bonga wrote music that addressed the questions of urban poverty and economic hardship under the colonial regime. His call for national independence made him a threat to the colonial regime. Indeed, his 1972 popular number "Mona Ki Ngi Xica," rendered in Kimbundu, was considered subversive by the colonial authority and earned him an arrest warrant.

Bonga, who was also a leading member of the MPLA, fled into exile in Rotterdam, the Netherlands, in 1966. As an exile in Europe, living at various times in Lisbon and Paris, Bonga continued to be engaged in political agitation and to employ his music in the service of the liberation struggle. During this period, he produced some of his most important records, including *Angola 72,* a collection of tracks along samba technique, and *Angola 74,* featuring a hint of Cape Verdean folk music, *morna,* and Congolese *soukouss.*

Although these albums launched him to international fame, access to them was limited in Angola during the colonial period. *Angola 72* was banned in Angola by the colonial authority, although it was illegally and clandestinely distributed.

Bonga continued to live abroad even after Angola's independence in 1975, but his music was never disconnected from the situation at home and traditional Angolan culture. Beyond Angola, his music has an international appeal, especially in the Lusophone world of Brazil, Mozambique, Cape Verde, and Guinea-Bissau. He has traveled extensively in the West, performing in several European capitals and even in the United States. Bonga continues to live in Portugal but records his albums with the Paris label LUSAFRICA.

Bonga is the doyen of Afro-pop music in Lusophone Africa. His music is conveyed in a sonorous tune yet with a sad quality reflective of the deplorable postcolonial situation in Angola. He continues to be a consistent social critic as his music often calls for social and political consciousness. His recent album, *Maiorais,* released in 2005, touches on persistent societal ills. In his career, he has recorded numerous Afro-pop albums, including recent popular ones like *Muelmba Xangola* and *Kaxexe,* and a compilation of his greatest hits, *O Melhor de Bonga.*

Another notable Angolan Afro-pop musician is Waldemar Bastos, who, like Bonga, has lived abroad for much of his career. After visiting the Eastern bloc states of Czechoslovakia, Poland, and the Soviet Union as well as Cuba, Bastos eventually settled in Brazil, a decision that shaped his musical career and gave a strong Brazilian flavor to his music. Later he went to settle in Lisbon, which in the 1990s was fast becoming an important center of Afro-Lusophone art and popular culture.

During the civil war, Bastos refused to be drawn into the conflict, remaining nonpartisan and focusing his music on what he called "a simple message, emphasizing the value of all life, the beauty and abundance of this world, and the profound need for hope."[3] Even though he does not live in Angola, he is incredibly popular at home. When he visited the country in 1990 and gave a free concert at Kinaxixe Square in Luanda, more than 200,000 people reportedly attended.[4]

Bastos's work combines elements of international and local influences: Portuguese *fado,* Brazilian samba, Congolese rhythms, and Angolan folk traditions. His first record, *Estamos Juntos* (We're Together), was produced in Brazil in 1986 in partnership with notable Brazilian singers Chico Buarque, Martinho Da Vila, and João do Vale. His first major work to receive wide acclaim was *Pretaluz,* released under the American label Luaka Bop, based in New York. His other important records are *Angola Minha Namorada, Pitanga Madura,* and *Renascence.*

Although Bonga and Bastos are ambassadors of Angolan music abroad, another notable musician, Elias DiaKiemuezo, held the home front. Regarded as the so-called king of Angolan music, DiaKiemuezo rose to prominence during the colonial period. His style of music is the *semba,* and his songs are usually in Kimbundu, unlike some Angolan artists, such as Bonga, who sing in other local languages and Portuguese.

Paulo Flores is another important Angolan musician who plays *semba* but who resides abroad and has had extensive overseas tours in Africa and in Europe. Relatively younger, born in 1972, Flores lives in Lisbon, where he has built a promising career as a leading Angolan musician with a formidable following. A singer with a gentle, soulful but penetrating voice, he produced his first album in 1988 at the age of 16. Despite his long sojourn abroad, his lyrics deal frankly with social issues in Angola such as the deplorable life of the average Angolan, political corruption, and the devastation caused by the war. Recording both in Portuguese and Kimbundu, Flores's most popular record is *Xé Povo.*

A few female musicians also have made their mark in the world of Angolan music. In the 1960s, Maria de Lourdes Pereira dos Santos Van-Dúnem became renowned and worked at various times with Ngola Ritmos and Orquestra os Jovens do Prenda. Her first album, *Monami,* was produced with Ngola Ritmos; thereafter she produced popular records like *Ser Mulher* and *Nzambi Kilamba.* She was a leading Angolan artist who was honored as the Queen of Angola's Female Voices at the Angolan Female Music Festival held in Luanda on August 2, 2003. As a singer of note, she performed not only within Angola but also outside the country in Portugal, Algeria, and Brazil. She was so popular in Angola that when she died in January 2006, President José Eduardo dos Santo attended her funeral.[5]

Equally important on the Angolan music scene is the female group As Gingas do Maculusso. This is a sensational group made up of young girls who have been referred to as the "Spice Girls" of Angola. When the group made its debut, the girls were practically children; today, they have blossomed into sensational adult singers with sweet, melodious, compelling, and captivating voices. One of the early performances of the group was the nursery rhyme "Mangonha" (Lazybones), which has today become very popular among Angolan children. During the civil war, As Gingas was known for rendering positive, uplifting songs of joy, peace, and encouragement in the midst of devastation. In recent times, the group has become an advocate of children's welfare in Angola, offering concerts to benefit disadvantaged children. The group is enormously popular throughout Angola and has represented the country in international music festivals. It has also performed in foreign countries such as Portugal, France, Italy, the United Kingdom, and

Brazil. The women are particularly known for their captivating stage shows and unique costumes.

A two-man group that has gained fame in the Angolan music industry is the Kafala Brothers. Moises and Jose Kafala acquired individual prominence as singers before coming together as a group in Luanda in 1987. Their music, reflecting the state of war-torn Angola and the realities of postwar challenges of national reconciliation, is a blend of traditional folk music and urban expressionism. The devastation of the Angolan war and the untold sufferings of the population are rendered in sad and poignant lyrics that evoke deep, powerful emotions in the listener. The Kafala Brothers' debut album is *Ngola* (after the Ndongo king), released in 1989. Their music also features Congolese, Brazilian, and Cuban rhythms.

Other Angolan musicians have made important contributions to the development of music in the country. They include André Mingas, Raul Ouro Negro, Filipe Mukenga, Mito Gaspar, Eduardo Paim, Ruka Vandunen, Miguel Zau, Teta Lando, Patrícia Faria, and Murtala de Oliveira (Dog Murras). A relatively new yet promising rap/hip-hop group is the Kalibrados, formed in 2002, whose debut album, *Negócio Fechado,* was released in 2005.

Foreign Influences on Angolan Music

Angolan music has an international quality. This stems from historical and contemporary cultural exchanges between Angola and the Caribbean and Latin America. The Atlantic slave trade established the first cultural connections between the two regions. Many of the slaves exported from the Luandan coast were taken to the Caribbean and South America. These enslaved Africans took with them to the New World many aspects of their African culture, including music. Thus, Brazilian and Cuban rhythms have been greatly influenced by Angolan traditional music.[6]

Brazil and Cuba have, in turn, impacted Angolan contemporary music. A number of notable Angolan musicians who had lived in Brazil adopted elements of the country's music. Some, like enterprising musician Bastos, recorded in partnership with leading Brazilian singers. The music of popular Angolan musician André Mingas also bear some traces of Afro-Cuban music. The principal Cuban influence on Angolan contemporary music arrived when Fidel Castro sent thousands of Cuban troops to Angola to assist the Marxist MPLA government during the civil war. The Cubans brought their musical culture to Angola, particularly the rumba drums.

Angolans themselves enjoy modern foreign music, from American pop, blues, jazz, and hip-hop to Jamaican reggae. It is part of youth culture in Angola to listen and dance at parties, bars, clubs, and cafés to world-class artists such as reggae superstar Bob Marley and pop icon Michael Jackson. In the immediate postindependence period, the liberation music of the Nigerian Afro-reggae musician Sonny Okosun and his *ozzidi* band was quite popular in the country and, indeed, in all of southern Africa. Many in Angola identified with his relentless call for the liberation of southern African states from oppressive white supremacist regimes. In popular albums such as "Fire in Soweto" and "Who Owns Papa's Land," Okosun deplored the brutality against the black population in southern Africa and sang of liberation.

Avenues of Musical Expression

Although modern Angolan music is present all over the nation, it is in the urban areas that it has had its greatest expression. Urban populations, particularly educated people and youth, are more receptive to Angolan popular music. The urban centers have hosted large concerts featuring many of the renowned musicians and drawing large crowds of people. Urban nightlife also has promoted Angolan music. Some nightclubs feature small-time local bands and disc jockeys play famous artists.

Many aspiring Angolan musicians have a problem recording their music. During the civil war, the limited recording infrastructure crumbled. Although the situation has improved since the end of the war, the facilities are inadequate to serve the industry. Many artists are therefore forced to seek recording opportunities in Europe and the United States. These opportunities are often better available to Angolan musicians based in Europe. Thus, the music of leading artists is more widely distributed outside Angola. Musicians like Bonga, Flores, and others sell their CDs in online Internet music stores. At home, record sales for many musicians are not impressive enough to sustain a living exclusively from music. Copyright laws are not respected, and illegal distribution of records is rampant, as aptly put by Flores: "Piracy is a real problem for our music, I remember being stuck in a traffic jam in Angola and a small boy trying to sell me a bootleg of my own disc!"[7]

The media have traditionally offered little support for musicians. Until recently, radio and television were more apt to play foreign music, particularly U.S. hits. In general, Angola's long-term economic and political uncertainty has not allowed many aspiring musicians to flourish. Many up-and-coming musicians have fled to neighboring countries, particularly South Africa, residing in major cities like Johannesburg and Cape Town and trying to make a living and support their music careers through odd jobs. South Africa, however, provided them greater opportunities to perform, collaborate, and record than Angola ever could.

Music and War

Music permeates and plays an important role in all areas of life in Angola. Even in a war situation, Angolans did not cease to employ music as an important weapon of war and peace. The use of music as a mobilizing force found expression during the war of liberation against Portuguese colonialism. Modern Angolan music in the late colonial era was revolutionary and supportive of the anticolonial movement. Its message was explicitly a call for political consciousness aimed at mobilizing the Angolan population behind the course of self-determination and national independence. With lyrics such as "Vai, vai te embo-ra / Isso assim não pode ser" (Go, go away / This situation cannot be),[8] the song "Milhoro" by the group Os Kiezos, which calls for the departure of the Portuguese, was banned by the colonial authority.

MPLA songs sung mostly in indigenous languages during the liberation war are the epitome of revolutionary music. These songs are an excursion into Angolan history and describe the glorious precolonial age, the rude Portuguese intervention through trickery, African heroic resistance, and the oppressive colonial epoch. Although they also lionized the MPLA, the songs were specifically directed at condemning the Portuguese and assuring Angolans that *victoria è certa!* (victory is certain!) in the current struggle.[9]

Angolans also expressed and described their situation during the long, brutal civil war that followed independence in 1975. Leading Angolan musicians sang about the war, the devastation it brought to people, and the need for peace. A major musical event of the late war period was the production of a joint peace album by a number of leading Angolan musicians. This project was based on the model offered by the 1985 multiartist single "We Are the World," written by Michael Jackson and Lionel Richie, to raise relief funds for famine-devastated Ethiopia. In April 1997, Luanda's office of Search for Common Ground, an international nongovernmental organization dedicated to conflict resolution, brought together 35 of Angola's most popular musicians to produce a peace song. Although they individually supported different sides in the conflict, these musicians, among whom were noted icons like Filipe Zau, Bonga, and Filipe Mukenga, shed their political and ideological differences to record the peace song "A paz e que O Povo Chama" (The People Are Calling for Peace). Produced in Lisbon, the song was officially launched in Luanda on August 30, 1997, at a well-attended peace concert held at Karl Marx Stadium. The song was an important vehicle for peace in Angola. It was a symbol of the possibility of reconciliation between seemingly irreconcilable factions. It became very popular, was broadcast on radio waves everywhere, and constituted something of a national song. Its success led to the organization of more peace concerts.

MUSICAL INSTRUMENTS

Musical instruments come in various forms, shapes, and sizes, and Angolan musicians have used every form, both traditional and modern, in their musical productions.[10] Although contemporary musicians no longer use many types of traditional instruments, these instruments were once the foundations of the rich Angolan musical tradition. Traditional instruments that perform the same musical functions are known by different names among the various ethnolinguistic groups. They also differ in size and shape yet function essentially the same.

In the past, most instruments were made by the musicians themselves. Generally, instruments are made out of local materials. For instance, the *dikanza,* a percussion instrument, is made out of grooved bamboo, and the *kisanji,* a handheld harmonic instrument is made from metal sheets. An instrument also could be fashioned out of animal parts, such as the *xingufo,* which is made from an antelope's horn. Instruments are generally decorated with local materials typical of the culture. Decoration materials may include gourds, shell pieces, beads, ironwork and brass, and metal rings.

Traditional musical instruments may be divided into four general categories. First, in the ideophone category, are percussion instruments made from resonating materials that do not require tuning. Examples of such instruments are the large Chokwe slit gongs *(chikuvu);* the marimba, a xylophone also popular among the Chokwe; and the *clochas* (double bell). Second, membraphonic instruments include the goatskin-covered drums *(ngoma).* Other types include the *ochingufo,* the Umbundu slit drum. A unique type is the friction drum variously known as *puita, kwita,* or *mpwita,* which produces sound not as a result of hitting the skin-covered end but by friction caused by a wet finger rubbed over it. The *puita* originated among the Kongo and is said to be the precursor of the Brazilian *cuica* and likely introduced to the New World by enslaved Africans from the Kongo region. The third category is chordophones, stringed instruments in which tension strings are attached to resonators made from wood or metal. An example of a string instrument is the *hungu* (or the *mbulumbumba*), popular among the Khoisan and thought to be the ancestor of the Brazilian *berimbau,* used in the capoeira dance. Other stringed instruments are the *kakocha,* the *tchihumba,* and the Umbundu *sansa.* The fourth category of instruments is wind or aerophonic instruments, which includes trumpets, horns, and flutes. Traditional wind instruments are the Kikongo trumpetlike *mpungu* and the *vandumbu,* used by the Ambwels. The *mjemboerose* is made from antelope's horn and common among the Herreo.

In addition to general musical use, some instruments also are used for specific musical purposes. The sounds of some instruments are suitable for funeral dirges *(komba di tokwa)*, and the drumbeat is a vital part of village festivals. The esoteric sound of the *xingufo* is suitable for spiritual songs during ritual ceremonies and spirit or ancestral worship. Among the Yaka and many ethnolinguistic groups, slit gongs are usually used during diviners' rites of initiation, and their intricate rhythm is supposed to conjure the necessary spiritual powers. In the social context, the *kisanji* typically provides the background sound for open-fire or moonlit stories told by elders.

Traditional instruments are for the most part no longer in use in Angola. Modern artists use the most common instruments of today, such as drums, guitars, flutes, trumpets, saxophones, keyboards, and others.

Dance

Forms of Music and Dance

The passion for dancing in Angola is expressed in different musical forms and dance styles. Many musicians still play traditional forms of music that quite often are combined with modern music. Whatever the form of music, Angolans love to dance, from traditional ritual dances to modern, high-tech disco.

In the contemporary period, opportunities abound to dance: at home with friends and relatives to blaring sound machines, at street parties and nightclubs to a live band playing local numbers, or to funk, rock, or pop records played by a disc jockey. A person even may be observed swaying to the beat of a car radio in a traffic jam.

Angolans have different dance styles, ranging from group dances to the sensuous *dance-à-deux.* Young people are adept in dance forms that require high-energy moves and wild shaking of hips and belly. Older people are more at home with a relaxed, slow form of dance. Some dance forms are even erotic, whereby dancers thrust their hips back and forth in a provocative manner. The major music and dance types are discussed in the following sections.

Kuduru

Kuduru is a form of hip-hop mixed with local rhythms that is popular in urban areas, particularly in the *musseques* of Luanda. It is a fast-paced, energetic form of dance to which Angolan youths are very receptive. One of the most popular musicians of *kuduru* is Dog Murras. The band Army Squad and the solo artist Mutu Moxy, both based in Cape Town, also play *kuduru.* The South Side Posse (SSP) is also one of the most successful hip-hop bands playing *kuduru.* Some of these musicians and groups render their lyrics in Portuguese, others in local Angolan languages.

Semba

Perhaps, the most popular dance form in Angola is the *semba*. This is high-tempo dance, somewhat sensuous, in which dance partners touch each other by the forward thrust of their bellies. *Semba* is said to have originated as a dance in celebration of special events such as births, marriages, and good harvests. The subject matter of *semba* music covers a whole range of social issues relating to everyday life. The dance originated and developed in the seventeenth century in the coastal areas of Angola around Luanda and Benguela.

It is widely believed that Angola's *semba* gave birth to the Brazilian national music, samba, through the enslaved Africans who carried it to Brazil by way of the transatlantic slave trade in the seventeenth century. Many Angolan musicians play the samba, often with instruments such as *tarolas* (can beats) and *dilongas* (basin). Some of the best modern innovators of *semba* are DiaKiemuezo and Bonga, the later being instrumental in the international popularization of the music. Before independence, *semba* was more popular in Angola than in contemporary times. Younger artists and groups, however, are joining veteran *semba* musicians to reclaim the style's old popularity. Examples are Flores and Maravilha, a band formed in the early 1990s.

Kizomba and Tarachinha

Kizomba and *tarachinha* are similar dance forms, more intimate, sensuous, and slower than *semba*. Like *semba*, *kizomba* is normally danced with a partner in a light embrace. Conflicting notions exist regarding the origins of *kizomba*. Although some contend that it is of Angolan origin with influences from other Lusophone countries, others hold that it originated on the Cape Verde Islands. Whatever its origins, *kizomba* is known throughout Lusophone Africa and in Portugal, particularly in Lisbon and its suburbs that have immigrant communities. In fact, *kizomba* is usually sung in Portuguese with African rhythms. Angolan musicians who play *kizomba* include Flores, Paim, Murras, Irmãos Verdade, and Don Kikas.

Tarachinha is an even more seductive dance than *kizomba*. Dancing partners are locked in a rather tight, sensual embrace and dance in a very slow manner, almost not moving. It is typically popular among younger Angolans.

Other Dance Forms

Capoeira de Angola is a martial art and acrobatic dance form that is more identified with Brazil than Angola. It is a popular Brazilian national tradition that originated in the sixteenth century among enslaved Africans who came to Brazil from Angola and the Kongo area. The dance, accompanied by music played with traditional instruments, was a way by which enslaved Africans confronted slavery. In its original form, resistance to slavery through actual physical fighting was hidden behind the cloak of dance.

Some claim that capoeira de Angola previously had existed in Angola and that, indeed, it was practiced in precolonial times but was banned by the Portuguese colonialists. Since then, it has not been a popular cultural tradition in Angola. Efforts have been made in recent times to revive the practice, however.

Both the *kabetula* and the *kazukuta* are other popular traditional dance forms in Angola. The *kabetula* is a fast waddle dance punctuated by acrobatic leaps, whereas the *kazukuta* is a slow tap dance accompanied by wild arm swings.

Carnival

Luanda's Mardi Gras parade is one of the most important cultural events in Angola. It is a three-day carnival that Angolans look forward to and that draws a very large crowd. It features the parade of *grupos carnavalescos* (carnival groups), drawn from Luanda and its neighborhoods and slum areas, who compete for prizes based on the quality of their dance and music. The groups are colorfully attired, some in masks and others in decorated headgear. They march to different music backed by wild drumming and dancing. During the carnival, Luanda turns into a sensuous city where people are engaged in a three-day spree of wild partying, alcohol abuse, and uninhibited sexual expression.

The carnival was inherited from the Portuguese with much infusion of African culture through costume and music. It was a very popular event in the 1960 and early 1970s, but the long postindependence civil war restricted its celebration, therefore diminishing its importance. Since the end of the war, Mardi Gras slowly has begun to reemerge as an Angolan festival of great splendor.

NOTES

1. Bastos, *Preta Luz.*
2. See Barlow, "Afropop Worldwide Visits Luanda, Angola."
3. Ibid.
4. Ibid.
5. "President dos Santos Pays Homage to Legendary Songstress."
6. For a discussion of the Angolan origins of Brazilian music, see Kubik, *Angolan Traits in Black Music, Games and Dances of Brazil.*
7. Cited in "More about Paulo Flores."
8. Cited in "Cool Rhythms."
9. See Brinkman, *Singing in the Bush.*
10. For a survey of Angolan musical instruments, see Redinha, *Instrumentos Musicais de Angola.*

Glossary

alambamento. Bridal gift offered by the groom's family to the bride's parents as part of traditional marriage rite.

assimilado. Africans during the colonial period who were assimilated into the Portuguese culture and theoretically acquired some privileges and rights of Portuguese citizenship.

bairros. Quarters.

calulu. Fish dish.

capoeira de Angola. Martial art and acrobatic dance form more identified with Brazil than Angola but originating from the latter.

catorzinhas. Term expressing sexual exploitation of young girls. It means, literally, "little 14-year-old," referring to the young age of sexually exploited girls.

caxi. Local alcoholic drink distilled from cassava and potato skins.

chibinda. Hunter.

chikuvu. Chokwe slit gong.

cihongo. Male mask of the Chokwe.

cikunza. Masquerade of the puberty rite among the Chokwe.

clientelismo. Practice whereby political leaders or party officials provide benefits or services in exchange for loyalty.

clochas. Double bell.

colonatos. Large agricultural settlements for white peasants who emigrated from Portugal and the Cape Verde Islands.

Cultura. Literary magazine issued in Luanda between 1957 and 1961, sponsored by the Angolan Cultural Society.

cultura nacional. Formulation of an Angolan national culture as espoused in the discourses of Angolan writers such as Agostinho Neto and Henrique Abranches.

degredado. Convicted criminals from Portugal sent to settle in Angola between the sixteenth and the early twentieth century.

dikanza. Musical instrument made out of grooved bamboo.

etambo. Spirit hut.

feiticeiros. Witches.

feiticismo. Practice of witchcraft.

fuli. Traditional blacksmiths.

funge. Corn flour pudding.

hungu, kakocha, sansa. Stringed musical instruments.

Ilunga Ketele. Lunda civilizing cultural hero, a hunter.

Imbangala. Marauding bands of warlike people who in the late sixteenth century allied with the Portuguese to expand the slave trade along the Luanda coast. Subsequently, they founded the kingdom of Kasanje.

indígenas. African unassimilated into the Portuguese culture during the colonial period and thus defined as native and considered uncivilized.

kabetula. Fast waddle dance punctuated by acrobatic leaps.

Kalunga. Supreme deity, the god of creation among the Chokwe.

kazukuta. Slow tap dance accompanied by wild arm swings.

kimbanda. Diviner or traditional healer who combines indigenous medical practice with the ability to consult the spirits.

kindoki. Evil spirits.

kisanji. Handheld harmonic instrument made from metal sheets.

kissangua **or** *ocissangua.* Corn-flour drink.

kizomba **and** *tarachinha.* Intimate, sensuous dance forms.

komba di tokwa. Funeral dirge.

kuduru. Urban-based hip-hop mixed with local rhythm.

kuimbo. Circular arrangement of huts in a compound.

kwanza. Angolan currency.

Lweji. Lunda female chief, the mythical wife of Ilunga, the civilizing cultural hero.

mahamba. Spirits of dead ancestors.

makishi. Mask worn during circumcision rites, popular among the Mbunda.

maluvu. Palm wine.

mancala. General name for board games common in many African societies. It is known by a variety of names in Angola, and is so popular that it is now a tournament attracting cash prizes up to $1,500 for winners.

Manikongo. Title of king of the precolonial state of Kongo.

marimba. Chokwe xylophone.

Mensagem. Luanda-based literary review published from 1951 to 1952.

mestiço. People of mixed European and African origins.

minkisi, nkisi (**singular**) Sacred statues of the Kongo.

mjemboerose. Antelope-horn wind instrument of the Herreo.

Mongozo. Chokwe traditional beer made from palm nuts.

morna. Folk music of Cape Verde.

mpungu. Kikongo trumpet.

Mtokoists. Members of the Angolan Our Lord Jesus Christ Church in the World.

muamba. Pepper- and garlic-seasoned chicken dish.

mufete de cacuso. Grilled fish dish.

mukanda. Male circumcision ritual.

musséques. Slums in Luanda.

muvalavala. Board game.

Mwana Pwo. Chokwe female ancestor.

ndemba. Mask used during initiation ceremonies for boys.

Negritude. Idea enunciated by Jonas Savimbi, former leader of the National Union for Total Independence of Angola (União Nacional para a Independência Total de Angola, UNITA). This is not to be confused with the more popular "negritude" espoused by Léopold Sédar Senghor, the former Senegalese president.

nganga. Diviner, among the Kongo.

Ngola. Title of the king of the Ndongo people that became the source of the name *Angola.*

ngoma. Goatskin-covered drums.

Nzambi. Supreme deity, the god of creation among the BaKongo.

ochingufo. Umbundu slit drum.

ociwo. Kitchen.

onjango. Parlor for hosting guests in a house.

osila. Barn for storage purposes.

Pensado. The *Thinker,* a popular Chokwe statue.

pombeiros. Slave trade agents who procured slaves from the interior.

puita, kwita, **or** *mpwita.* Friction drum.

semba. High-tempo, sensuous dance.

sobas. Traditional leader.

sona. Chokwe sand drawing.

songi. Professional carvers among the Chokwe.

soukouss. Congolese music.

tarolas and dilongas. Musical instruments.

tchihumba. A violin.

vandumbu. Wood trumpet used by the Ambwels.

wali. Chokwe female initiation rite.

wanga. Sorcerers among the Chokwe.

xingufo. Musical instrument made from an antelope's horn.

Bibliography

Abshire, David M., and Michael A. Samuels. "The Continuing Crisis in Angola." *Current History* 82, no. 482 (March 1983): 124–25, 128, 138.

———, eds. *Portuguese Africa: A Handbook* (New York: Praeger, 1969).

Adams, Gordon, and Michael Locker. "Cuba and Africa: The Politics of the Liberation Struggle." *Cuba Review* 8, no. 1 (October 1978): 3–9.

Adams, Tom. "Cuba in Angola: A Balance Sheet." *Military Intelligence* 8 (January–March 1982): 32–36.

Afolabi, Niyi. *Golden Cage: Regeneration in Lusophone African Literature and Culture* (Trenton, NJ: Africa World Press, 2001).

Agostinho Neto, Antonio. *A Renúncia Impossível* (Luanda: Angolan Writers Union, 1982).

Agostinho Neto, Antonio. *Sagrada Esperança* (Luanda: União dos Escritores Angolanos, 1979).

Aguilar, Renato. *Angola: A Long and Hard Way to the Marketplace* (Stockholm: Swedish International Development Authority, 1991).

Alao, George. "The Development of Lusophone African Literary Magazines." *Research in African Literatures* 30, no. 1 (spring 1999): 169–83.

Anderson, Allan A., and Gerald J. Pillay. "The Segregated Spirit: The Pentacostals." In *Christianity in South Africa: A Political, Social and Cultural History,* ed. Richard Elphick and Rodney Davenport (Berkeley and Los Angeles: University of California Press, 1997).

Andrade, F. *A Life of Improvisation: Displaced People in Malanje and Benguela* (Luanda: Development Workshop, 2001).

Angola, Manso Santos. "Angola: The Forgotten Victims." *Angola Today*, 301, no. 2 (February 29, 1996): 1.

"Angola Exports." *CIA World Factbook* (2005). Index Mundi, http://www.indexmundi.com/g/g.aspx?c=ao&v=85.

"Angola External Debt." *CIA World Factbook* (2005). Index Mundi, http://www.indexmundi.com/g/g.aspx?c=ao&v=94.

"Angola Imports." *CIA World Factbook* (2005). Index Mundi, http://www.indexmundi.com/g/g.aspx?c=ao&v=89.

"Angolan Artifact Stolen." *Museum Security Network* (December 4, 2001), http://www.museum-security.org/01/193.html.

ANGOP. http://www.angolapress-angop.ao/angop-e.asp.

Anstee, Margaret Joan. *Orphan of the Cold War: The Inside Story of the Collapse of the Angolan Peace Process, 1992–93* (New York: St. Martin's Press, 1996).

Ashcroft, Bill, Gareth Griffiths, and Helen Tiffin. *The Empire Writes Back: Theory and Practice in Post-Colonial Literatures* (New York: Routledge, 1989).

Axelson, Eric. *Portugal and the Scramble for Africa, 1875–1891* (Johannesburg: Witwatersrand University Press, 1967).

Balandier, George. *Daily Life in the Kingdom of the Kongo from the Sixteenth to the Eighteenth Century* (New York: World, 1969).

Banham, Martin, ed. *A History of Theatre in Africa* (Cambridge: Cambridge University Press, 2004).

Barlow, Sean. "Afropop Worldwide Visits Luanda, Angola." Afropop Worldwide, http://www. afropop.org/multi/feature/ID/561/Afropop+WorldWide+Visits+Angola.

Barnard, Alan. *Hunters and Herders of Southern Africa: A Comparative Ethnography of the Khoisan Peoples* (Cambridge: Cambridge University Press. 1992).

Bastin, Marie-Louise, "Chokwe Arts: Wealth of Symbolism and Aesthetic Expression." In *Chokwe! Art and Initiation among Chokwe and Related Peoples,* ed. Manuel Jordan (New York: Prestel, 1998).

———. "Musical Instruments, Songs and Dances of the Chokwe." *African Music* 7, no. 2 (1992): 23–44.

———. *Les Sculptures Tshokwe* (Meudon, France: Alain et Francoise Chaffin, 1982).

———. "Statuettes Tshokwe du Héros Civilisateur Tshibinda Ilunga: A propos de Statuettes Tshokwe Représentant un Chef Chasseur." In *Arts d'Afrique Noire,* ed. (Arnouville, France: Arts d'Afrique Noire, 1978).

Bastos, Waldemar. "Preta Luz," http://www.luakabop.com/waldemar/cmp/info.html.

Bauer, John. *2000 Years of Christianity in Africa: An African History, 62–1992* (Nairobi, Kenya: Paulines, 1994).

Bender, Gerald J. *Angola under the Portuguese: The Myth and the Reality* (Berkeley and Los Angeles: University of California Press, 1978).

Bhagavan, M. R. *Angola's Political Economy, 1975–1985* (Uppsala, Sweden: Scandinavian Institute of African Studies, 1986).

"Bié: Umpulo Population Faces Food Crisis." Angola Press Agency, September 4, 2003. http://www.angolapress-angop.ao/index-e.asp

Birkeland, N., and A. U. Gomes. "Angola: Deslocados in the Province of Huambo." In *Caught between Borders: Response Strategies of the Internally Displaced,* ed. Marc Vincent and Birgitte Refslund Sorensen (London: Pluto Press, 2001).

Birmingham, David. "The African Response to Early Portuguese Activities in Angola." In *Protest and Resistance in Angola and Brazil: Comparative Studies,* ed. Ronald H. Chilcote (Berkeley and Los Angeles: University of California Press, 1972).

———. *Frontline Nationalism in Angola and Mozambique* (Trenton, NJ: Africa World Press, 1992).

———. *The Portuguese Conquest of Angola* (London: Oxford University Press, 1965).

———. "Themes and Resources of Angolan History." *African Affairs* 73, no. 291 (April 1974): 188–203.

———. *Trade and Conflict in Angola: The Mbundu and Their Neighbours under the Influence of the Portuguese, 1483–1790* (Oxford: Clarendon Press, 1966).

Birmingham, David, and Phyllis M. Martin, eds. *History of Central Africa: The Contemporary Years since 1960* (New York: Longman, 1998).

Boonzaier, Emile, Candy Malherbe, Andy Smith, and Penny Berens. *The Cape Herders: A History of the Khoikhoi of Southern Africa* (Athens: Ohio University Press, 1996).

Boxer, Charles Ralph. *The Portuguese Seaborne Empire, 1415–1825* (London: Hutchinson, 1969).

Brinkman, Inge. "Language, Names, and War: The Case of Angola." *African Studies Review* 47, no. 3 (December 2004): 143–63.

———, ed. *Singing in the Bush: MPLA Songs during the War for Independence in South-East Angola, 1966–1975* (Cologne, Germany: Rüdiger Köppe, 2001).

Brinkman, Inge, and Axel Fleisch, eds. *Grandmother's Footsteps: Oral Tradition and South-East Angolan Narratives on the Colonial Encounter* (Cologne, Germany: Köppe, 1999).

Broadhead, Susan Herlin. *Historical Dictionary of Angola* (Metuchen, NJ: Scarecrow Press, 1992).

Brooke, James. "Cuba's Strange Mission in Angola." *New York Times Magazine,* February 1, 1987, 24, 28, 45, 47–48.

Bureau of Democracy, Human Rights, and Labor. "Country Reports on Human Rights Practices 2002," http://www.state.gov/g/drl/rls/hrrpt/2002/18167.htm.

Burness, Donald. *Critical Perspectives on Lusophone Literature from Africa* (Washington, DC: Three Continents Press, 1981).

———. *Fire: Six Writers from Angola, Mozambique, and Cape Verde* (Washington, DC: Three Continents Press, 1977).

———. *On the Shoulder of Marti: Cuban Literature of the Angolan War* (Boulder, CO: Lynne Rienner, 1996).

Capello, Guilherme Augusto de Brito. *Aspects of Angolan History* (Lisbon: Imprensa Nacional, 1989).

Castelo, Maria Antónia, Miguel Gaspan, and Balbina Ventura Félix. "A Cultural Approach to HIV/AIDS Prevention and Care: Angola's Experience." *UNESCO Special Series,* no. 4 (1999): 33–34.

Central Intelligence Agency. "Angola." *World Fact Book* (2006), https://www.cia.gov/cia/publications/factbook/geos/ao.html.

Chatelain, Héli, ed. *Folk-Tales of Angola: Fifty Tales with Kimbundu Text, Literal English Translation, Introduction, and Notes* (New York: Negro University Press, 1894).

Cheney, David M. "Angola Statistics by Province by Name." Catholic-Hierarchy.org, http://www.catholic-hierarchy.org/country/spcao4.html.

Chilcote, Ronald H., ed. *Protest and Resistance in Angola and Brazil: Comparative Studies* (Berkeley and Los Angeles: University of California Press, 1972).

Cilliers, Jakkie, and Christian Dietrich. *Angola's War Economy: The Role of Oil and Diamonds* (Pretoria, South Africa: Institute for Security Studies, 2000).

Ciment, James. *Angola and Mozambique: Postcolonial Wars in Southern Africa* (New York: Facts on File, 1997).

Clarence-Smith, W. G. *Slaves, Peasants, and Capitalists in Southern Angola, 1840–1926* (Cambridge: Cambridge University Press, 1979).

Colaço, Luis Filipe Sousa. *A situacao da mulher em Angola* (Luanda: OMA and Sida, 1990).

Committee to Protect Journalists. "Country Report: Angola" (31 December 1998), http://www.cpj.org/attacks98/1998/Africa/Angola.html.

"Cool Rhythms." *SANANGO Universo* no. 4 (winter 2004): 22.

Cox, Brian C., ed. *African Writers* (New York: Scribner, 1997).

Crowley, Daniel J. "An African Aesthetic." *Journal of Aesthetics and Art Criticism* 24, no. 4 (1966): 523.

Curtis, Valerie. *Water and Women's Work in Malanje, Angola* (London: London School of Hygiene and Tropical Medicine, 1988).

Dalby, David. *Language Map of Africa and the Adjacent Islands* (London: International African Institute, 1977).

Dathorne, O. R., and Willfried Feuser, eds. *Africa in Prose* (Baltimore: Penguin Books, 1969).

———. *African Literature in the Twentieth Century* (London: Heinemann, 1976).

———. *The Black Mind: A History of African Literature* (Minneapolis: University of Minnesota Press, 1974).

"Deputy Mass Media Minister on New Press Law." *Angola Press,* 1 September 2005, http://www.angolapress-angop.ao/noticia-e.asp?ID=370540.

Deutschmann, David. *Changing the History of Africa: Angola and Namibia* (North Melbourne, Australia: Ocean, 1991).

"Elections in Angola," *African Elections Database,* http://africanelections.tripod.com/ao.html#1992_Presidential_Election.

Elphick, Richard, and Rodney Davenport, eds. *Christianity in South Africa* (Berkeley and Los Angeles: University of California Press, 1997).

Ember, Melvin, and Carol R. Ember, eds. *Countries and Their Cultures* (Macmillan, 2001).

England, Nicholas M., *Music among the Zu'lwã-si and Related Peoples of Namibia, Botswana, and Angola* (New York: Garland, 1995).

Falk, Pamela S. "Cuba in Africa." *Foreign Affairs* 65, no. 5 (summer 1987): 1077–96.

Falola, Toyin. "Colonialism and Exploitation: The Case of Portugal in Africa." *Lusophone Area Studies Journal* 1, no. 1 (January 1983): 41–62.

"Family Minister Condemns Premature Marriage." *Angola Press Agency,* April 11, 2006, http://allafrica.com/stories/200604120149.html.

Furley, Oliver, ed. *Conflict in Africa* (London: I. B. Tauris, 1995).

Fyfe, Christopher, and Andrew Walls, eds. *Christianity in Africa in the 1990s* (Edinburgh: Centre of African Studies, University of Edinburgh, 1996).

Gaines, Kevin. *Uplifting the Race: Black Leadership, Politics, and Culture in the Twentieth Century* (Chapel Hill: University of North Carolina Press, 1996).

Geertz, C. *The Interpretation of Cultures* (New York: Basic Books, 1973).

Gerdes, Paulus. *Geometry from Africa: Mathematical and Educational Explorations* (Washington, DC: Mathematical Association of America, 1999).

Gillon, Werner. *Collecting African Art* (London: Studio Vista/Christie's, 1979).

Gomes, Aldónio, and Fernanda Cavacas. *Dicionàrio de Autores de Literaturas Africanas de Língua Portuguesa* (Lisbon: Editorial Caminho, 1997).

Green, Edward C., and Aleinda Honwana. "Indigenous Healing of War-Affected Children in Africa." *Africa Policy E-Journal* no. 10 (July 1999), http://www.africaaction.org/docs99/viol9907.htm.

Grenfell, James. "Simão Toco: An Angolan Prophet." *Journal of Religion in Africa* 28, no. 2 (May, 1998): 210–26.

Grohs, Gerhard, and Godehard Czernik. *State and the Church in Angola, 1450–1980* (Geneva: Institut universitaire de hautes études internationales, 1983).

Guimarães, Aniceto. "The Evils of Muzzled Press in Angola." *Angola Today,* February 29, 1996, 3–4.

Guimarães, Fernando Andresen. *The Origins of the Angolan Civil War: Foreign Intervention and Domestic Political Conflict* (New York: St. Martin's Press, 1998).

Habgood, L. *Health and Livelihoods in Rural Angola: A Participatory Research Project* (Oxford: Oxfam, 1999).

Hafner, Dorinda. *A Taste of Africa: Traditional and Modern African Cooking* (Berkeley, CA: Ten Speed Press, 2002).

Hambly, Wilfried D. *The Ovimbundu of Angola* (Chicago: Field Museum of History, 1934).

Hamilton, Cherie Y. *Cuisines of Portuguese Encounters: Recipes from Portugal, Madeira/Azores, Guinea-Bissau, Cape Verde, São Tomé and Príncipe, Angola, Mozambique, Goa, Brazil, Malacca, East Timor, and Macao* (New York: Hippocrene Books, 2001).

Hamilton, Russell G. *Literatura Africana, Literatura Necessària, Vol. 1: Angola* (Lisbon: Edições 70, 1981).

———. *Voices from an Empire: A History of Afro-Portuguese Literature* (Minneapolis: University of Minnesota Press, 1975).

Hare, Paul. *Angola's Last Best Chance for Peace: An Insider's Account of the Peace Process* (Washington, DC: United States Institute of Peace Press, 1998).

Harris, Jessica B. *The Africa Cookbook: Tastes of a Continent* (New York: Simon & Schuster, 1998).

Hart, Keith, and Joanna Lewis, eds. *Why Angola Matters* (Cambridge: University of Cambridge, 1995).

Hastings, Adrian. *African Catholicism: Essays in Discovery* (Philadelphia: Trinity Press International, 1989).

Heimer, Franz-Wilhelm, ed. *Social Change in Angola* (Munich: Weltforum Verlag, 1973).

Henderson, Lawrence W. *Angola: Five Centuries of Conflict* (Ithaca, NY: Cornell University Press, 1990).

———. *The Church in Angola: A River of Many Currents* (Cleveland: Pilgrim Press, 1992).

———. *Development and the Church in Angola: Jesse Chipenda, the Trailblazer* (Nairobi: Acton Publishers, 2000).

———. *Galangue: The Unique Story of a Mission Station in Angola Proposed, Supported, and Staffed by Black Americans* (New York: United Church Board for World Ministries, 1986).

Herrick, Allison Butler. *Area Handbook for Angola* (Washington, DC: U.S. Government Printing Office, 1967).

Hilton, Ann. *The Kingdom of the Kongo* (Oxford: Oxford University Press, 1985).

Hodges, Tony. *After Angola: The War over Southern Africa* (New York: Africana, 1976).

———. *Angola: Anatomy of an Oil State* (Bloomington: Indiana University Press, 2004).

———. *Angola from Afro-Stalinism to Petro-Dollar Capitalism* (Bloomington: Indiana University Press, 2001).

Honwana, Alcinda, *Child Soldiers in Africa* (Philadelphia: University of Pennsylvania Press, 2006).

———. "Non-Western Concepts of Mental Health," *The Refugee Experience,* http://earlybird.qeh.ox.ac.uk/rfgexp/rsp_tre/student/nonwest/toc.htm.

———. "*Okusiakala ondalo yokalye,* Let us Light the New Fire: Local Knowledge in the Post-War Healing and Reintegration of War-Affected Children in Angola." *Consultancy Report for the Christian Children Fund* 22 (1998), http://www.forcedmigration.org/psychosocial/inventory/pwg001/.

Hultman, Tami, ed. *The Africa News Cookbook: African Cooking for Western Kitchens* (New York: Penguin, 1986).

Human Rights Watch. *Angola Unravels: The Rise and Fall of the Lusaka Peace Process* (New York: Human Rights Watch, 1999).

Hurlich, Susan. *Angola: Country Gender Analysis,* 2 vols. (Luanda: Development Workshop, 1991).

Infoplease. "Angola." http://www.infoplease.com/ipa/A0107280.html

Inikori, Joseph. "Africa and the Trans-Atlantic Slave Trade." In *Africa Volume I: Africa before 1885*, ed. Toyin Falola (Durham, NC: Carolina Academic Press, 2000).

International Lesbian and Gay Association. *World Legal Survey: Angola* (1999), http://www.ilga.info/Information/Legal_survey/africa/angola.htm.

Irele, Abiola, and Simon Gikandi, eds. *The Cambridge History of African and Caribbean Literature* (Cambridge: Cambridge University Press, 2004).

Isichei, Elizabeth. *A History of Christianity in Africa from Antiquity to the Present* (Lawrenceville, NJ: Africa World Press, 1995).

Jacobs, Sylvia M., ed. *Black Americans and the Missionary Movement in Africa* (Westport, CT: Greenwood Press, 1982).

Johnson, Lillie M. "Missionary-Government Relations: Black Americans in British and Portuguese Colonies." In *Black Americans and the Missionary Movement in Africa,* ed. Sylvia M. Jacobs (Westport, CT: Greenwood Press, 1982).

Jordán, Manuel, ed. *Chokwe! Art and Initiation among Chokwe and Related Peoples* (New York: Prestel, 1998).

———. *The Kongo Kingdom* (New York: Franklin Watts, 1999).

Kandjimbo, Luís. "Verbetes: de escretories Angolanos," http://www.nexus.ao/kandjimbo/index_escritores.htm.

Kleinman, Arthur. *Patients and Healers in the Context of Culture: An Exploration of the Borderland between Anthropology, Medicine, and Psychiatry* (Berkeley and Los Angeles: University of California Press, 1980).

Kubik, Gerhard. *Angolan Traits in Black Music, Games and Dances of Brazil: A Study of African Cultural Extensions Overseas* (Lisbon: Junta de Investigações Científicas do Ultramar, 1979).

———. "Likembe Tunings of Kufuna Kandonga (Angola)." *African Music* 6, no. 1 (1980): 70–88.

Labode, Modupe. "'A Native Knows a Native': African American Missionaries' Writings about Angola, 1919–1940." *The North Star* 4, no. 1 (fall 2000): 1–14.

Labuschagne, Gerhardus Stephanus. *Moscow, Havana and the MPLA Takeover of Angola* (Pretoria, South Africa: Foreign Affairs Association, 1976).

Lauré, Jason. *Angola: Enchantment of the World* (Chicago: Children's Press, 1990).

Leakey, M. D., and L.S.B. Leakey. *Some String Figures from North East Angola* (Lisbon: Musea Do Dondo, 1949).

Legum, Colin. "The Soviet Union, China, and the West in Southern Africa." *Foreign Affairs* 54 no. 4 (July 1976): 745–62.

Leite, Ana Mafalda. "Angola." In *The Post-Colonial Literature of Lusophone Africa,* ed. Patrick Chabal (Evanston, IL: Northwestern University Press, 1996).

Lovejoy, Paul. *Transformations in Slavery: A History of Slavery in Africa* (Cambridge: Cambridge University Press, 2000).

Luke-Boone, Ronke. *African Fabrics* (Iola, WI: Krause, 2001).

Macqueen, Norrie. *The Decolonization of Portuguese Africa: Metropolitan Revolution and the Dissolution of Empire* (New York: Longman, 1997).

Maier, Karl. *Angola: Promises and Lies* (Rivonia, South Africa: W. Waterman, 1996).

Mann, Kenny. *West Central Africa: Kongo, Ndongo* (Parsippany, NJ: Dillon Press, 1996).

Marques, Rafael. "The Lipstick of Dictatorship." *Agora,* July 3, 1999, http://www.afrol.com/Countries/Angola/backgr_marques_santos.htm.

McCulloch, Merran. *The Ovimbundu of Angola* (London: International African Institute, 1952).

————. *The Southern Lunda and Related Peoples* (London: International African Institute, 1951).

McKissack, Pat. *Nzingha: Warrior Queen of Matamba* (New York: Scholastic, 2000).

Mendes, Pedro Rosa. *Bay of Tigers: An African Odyssey through War-Torn Angola* (San Diego: Harcourt, 2003).

Mendiluce, José María. *Luanda* (Barcelona: Planeta, 2001).

Messiant, Christine. "Angola: The Challenge of Statehood." In *History of Central Africa: The Contemporary Years since 1960,* ed. David Birmingham and Phyllis M. Martin (New York: Longman, 1998).

Miller, Joseph Calder. *Kings and Kinsmen: Early Mbundu States in Angola* (Oxford: Clarendon Press, 1976).

————. *Way of Death: Merchant Capitalism and the Angolan Slave Trade, 1730–1830* (Madison: University of Wisconsin Press, 1988).

Minter, William. *Apartheid's Contras: An Inquiry into the Roots of War in Angola and Mozambique* (London: Zed Books, 1994).

Mitras, Luís. "Theatre in Portuguese Speaking African Countries." In *A History of Theatre in Africa,* ed. Martin Banham (Cambridge: Cambridge University Press, 2004).

Monteiro, Ramiro Ladeiro. "From Extended to Residual Family: Aspects of Social Change in the *musséques* of Luanda." In *Social Change in Angola,* ed. Franz-Wilhelm Heimer (Munich: Weltforum Verlag, 1973).

Moorman, Marissa. "Dueling Bands and Good Girls: Gender and Music in Luanda's Musseques, 1961–74." *International Journal of African Historical Studies* 37, no. 2 (2004): 255–88.

————. "Of Westerns, Women and War: Resituating Angolan Cinema and the Nation." *Research in African Literature* 32, no. 3 (fall 2001): 103–22.

————. "Putting on a Pano and Dancing like Our Grandparents: Dress and Nation in Late Colonial Luanda." In *Fashioning Africa: Power and the Politics of Dress,* ed. Jean Allman (Bloomington: Indiana University Press, 2004).

"More about Paulo Flores." *Palop Africa,* http://www.palopafrica.co.uk/palop/scene/paulo.html.

Moser, Gerald M. *Essays in Portuguese-African Literature* (University Park: Pennsylvania State University Press, 1969).

Moser, Gerald, and Manuel Ferreira. *A New Bibliography of the Lusophone Literatures of Africa* (London: Hans Zell, 1993).

Mourão, Fernando Augusto Albuquerque. *A Sociedade Angolana Através da Literatura* (São Paulo, Brazil: Editora Ática 1978).

Neighbour, Margaret. "Half of Angola's Children Malnourished, UN Warns." *The Scotsman,* September 20, 2005, http://news.scotsman.com/topics.cfm?tid=666&id=1964632005.

Neto, Agostinho. *Sagrada Esperança* (Luanda: União dos Escritores Angolanos, 1979).

Nidel, Richard. *World Music: The Basics* (New York: Routledge, 2005).

Njoku, Onwuka N. *Mbundu* (New York: Rosen, 1997).

Nordstrom, Carolyn. *A Different Kind of War Story* (Philadelphia: University of Pennsylvania Press, 1997).

Olupona, Jacob K., ed. *African Traditional Religion in Contemporary Society* (New York: International Religious Foundation, 1991).

Organização da Mulher Angola. *Liberation in Southern Africa: The Organization of Angolan Women* (Chicago: Chicago Committee for the Liberation of Angola, Mozambique, and Guinea, 1976).

Owomoyela, Oyekan. "African Literature." *Microsoft Encarta Online Encyclopedia* (2005), http://encarta.msn.com/encyclopedia_761555353_1/African_Literature.html.

Oyebade, Adebayo. "Radical Nationalism and Wars of Liberation." In *Africa, Vol.4: Colonial Rule, Nationalism, and Decolonization,* ed. Toyin Falola (Durham, NC: Carolina Academic Press, 2000).

Paris, Roland. *At War's End: Building Peace after Civil Conflict* (Cambridge: Cambridge University Press, 2004).

"Parliament Passes Law on Freedom of Conscience, Worship, Religion." *Angola Press,* 31 May 2004, http://www.angolapress-angop.ao/noticia-e.asp?ID=255374.

"People Are Calling for Peace." *People Building Peace,* http://www.gppac.net/documents/pbp/5/4_radio_.htm.

Pepetela. *Yaka.* Trans. Marga Holness (Oxford: Heinemann, 1996).

Peres, Phyllis. *Transculturation and Resistance in Lusophone African Narrative* (Gainesville: University Press of Florida, 1997).

Permanent Mission of the Republic of Angola to the United Nations. Newsletter no. 11 (February 2005), http://www.un.int/angola/newsletter11.htm.

Ponte, Bruno da. *The Last to Leave: Portuguese Colonialism in Africa* (London: International Defence and Aid Fund, 1974).

Prendergast, John. *Angola's Deadly War: Dealing with Savimbi's Hell on Earth* (Washington, DC: United States Institute of Peace, 1999).

"President dos Santos Pays Homage to Legendary Songstress." *Angola Press Agency,* 6 January 2006. Cited in "Maria de Lourdes Pereira dos Santos Van-Dúnem," Wikipedia, the Free Encyclopedia, http://en.wikipedia.org/wiki/Maria_de_Lourdes_Pereira_dos_Santos_Van-D%C3%BAnem.

Pretorius, Hennie, and Lizo Jafta. "A Branch Springs Out: African Initiated Churches." In *Christianity in South Africa,* ed. Richard Elphick and Rodney Davenport (Berkeley and Los Angeles: University of California Press, 1997).

Raboteau, Albert J. *A Fire in the Bones: Reflections on African-American Religious History* (Boston: Beacon Press, 1995).

Redinha, José. *Instrumentos Musicais de Angola: Sua Construção e descrição: Notas Históricas e Etno-Sociológicas da Música Angolana* (Coimbra, Portugal: Instituto de Antropologia, 1984).

———. *Paredes Pintadas da Lunda* (Lisbon: Companhia de Diamantes de Angola, 1953).

Reis, Roberto, ed. *Toward Socio-Criticism: Selected Proceedings of the Conference "Luso-Brazilian Literatures, a Socio-Critical Approach"* (Tempe, AZ: Center for Latin American Studies, 1991).

Republic of Angola. *Newsletter of the Embassy of Angola in the UK.* No. 101 (December 2004/January 2005), http://www.angola.org.uk/newsletter101.htm.

Republic of Angola. *Newsletter of the Embassy of Angola in the UK.* No. 102 (February 2005), http://www.angola.org.uk/newsletter102.htm.

Reynolds, Pamela. *Traditional Healers and Childhood in Zimbabwe* (Athens: Ohio University Press, 1996).

Richter, Linda, Andrew Dawes, Craig Higson-Smith. *Sexual Abuse of Young Children in Southern Africa* (Cape Town: HSRC Press, 2004).

Rodney, Walter. "European Activity and African Resistance in Angola." In *Aspects of Central African History,* ed. T. O. Tanger (Evanston, IL: Northwestern University Press, 1970).

Rodrigues, Jose Honorio. *Brazil and Africa* (Berkeley and Los Angeles: University of California Press, 1965).

Ruigrok, Inge. "Angolan Cinema Flourishes after the War." *Power of Culture,* Cinema of Africa, http://www.powerofculture.nl/uk/specials/cinema_in_africa/angola.html.

Ruigrok, Inge. "Art in the 'New' Angola." *Current Affairs* (September 2003), http://www. powerofculture.nl/uk/current/2003/september/benguela.html.

Sanders, W. H. *A Collection of Umbundu Proverbs, Adages and Conundrums from Angola* (n.p.: American Board of Commissioners of Foreign Missions, 1914).

Santos, Naiole Cohen dos. *Beyond Inequalities: Women in Angola* (Harare, Zimbabwe: Southern African Research and Documentation Centre, 2000).

Schaider, J., S. Ngonyani, S. Tomlin, R. Rydman, and R. Roberts. "International Maternal Mortality Reduction: Outcome of Traditional Birth Attendant Education and Intervention in Angola." *Journal of Medical Systems* 23, no. 2 (April 1999): 99–105.

Schechter, Danny. "The Havana-Luanda Connection." *Cuba Review* 6 (March 1976): 5–13.

Sheehan, Sean. *Angola* (New York: M. Cavendish, 1999).

Shorter, Aylward. "The Roman Catholic Church in Africa Today." In *Christianity in Africa in the 1990s,* ed. Christopher Fyfe and Andrew Walls (Edinburgh: Centre of African Studies, University of Edinburgh, 1996).

Simoes da Silva, Tony. *A Bibliography of Lusophone Women Writers,* http://www.arts.uwa.edu. au/AFLIT/FEMECalireLU.html.

Smith, Edwin William, ed. *African Ideas of God: A Symposium* (London: Edinburgh House Press, 1950).

————. *The Christian Mission in Africa* (London: International Missionary Council, 1926).

Somerville, Keith. *Angola: Politics, Economics, and Society* (Boulder, CO: L. Rienner, 1986).

Soremekun, Fola. "A History of the American Board Mission in Angola, 1880–1940." PhD dissertation, Northwestern University, 1965.

Stanley, Janet L. *African Art: A Bibliographic Guide* (New York: Africana, 1985).

Steyn, Hendrik Pieter. *Vanished Lifestyles: The Early Cape Khoi and San* (Pretoria, South Africa: Unibook, 1990).

Suarez, Virgil. *Spared Angola: Memories from a Cuban-American Childhood* (Houston: Arte Público Press, 1997).

Sweet, James H. *Recreating Africa: Culture, Kingship, and Religion in the African-Portuguese World, 1441–1770* (Chapel Hill: University of North Carolina Press, 2003).

Thornton, John. "The Development of an African Catholic Church in the Kingdom of Kongo, 1491–1750." *Journal of African History* 25 (1984): 147–67.

————. *Kongolese Saint Anthony: Dona Beatriz Kimpa Vita and the Antonian Movement, 1684–1706* (Cambridge: Cambridge University Press, 1998).

"Trade with Angola: 2003," U.S. Census Bureau, Foreign Trade Division, Data Dissemination Branch (Washington, DC: 2003), http://www.census.gov/foreign-trade/balance/ c7620.html#2003.

Tucker, John Taylor. *Drums in the Darkness* (New York: George H. Doran, 1927).

Tvedten, Inge. *Angola: Struggle for Peace and Reconstruction* (Boulder, CO: Westview, 1997).

UN Office for the Coordination of Humanitarian Affairs. "Angola: Children Ravaged by War." *Integrated Regional Information Networks (IRIN),* February 1, 2005, http:// www.irinnews.org/report.asp?ReportID=43401.

Van der Waals, Willem S. *Portugal's War in Angola, 1961–1974* (Rivonia, South Africa: Ashanti, 1993).

Walker, John Frederick. *A Certain Curve of Horn: The Hundred-Year Quest for the Giant Sable Antelope of Angola* (New York: Atlantic Monthly Press, 2002).

Wallace, Emma, and Peter Sinclair. *Art from the Frontline: Contemporary Art from Southern Africa: Angola, Botswana, Mozambique, Tanzania, Zambia, Zimbabwe* (London: Frontline States/Karia Press, 1990).

Werner, Alice. *Myths and Legends of the Bantu* (London: Cass, 1968).

Wheeler, Douglas L., and René Pélissier. *Angola* (New York: Praeger, 1971).

Wikipedia. "Roman Catholicism by Country." Answers.com, http://www.answers.com/topic/roman-catholics-by-country.

Williams, Walter. *Black Americans and the Evangelization of Africa, 1877–1900* (Madison: University of Wisconsin Press, 1982).

Wolfers, Michael. *Poems from Angola* (London: Heinemann Educational Books, 1979).

World Food Program/Vulnerability Analysis and Mapping. *Food Security and Livelihood Survey in the Central Highlands of Rural Angola* (2005), http://www.wfp.org/country_brief/africa/angola/docs/Food_Security_and_Livelihood_Survey_in_CH_June_2005.pdf.

"World Military Expenditures and Arms Transfers, 1998," U.S. Arms Control and Disarmament Agency, http://www.globalsecurity.org/military/world/spending.htm.

World Vision UK. "Angola: A Tangled Web, Many Players in a Complex War" (July 2000), http://www.worldvision.org.uk/resources/angolareport.pdf.

Index

About the Author

ADEBAYO O. OYEBADE is Associate Professor of History at Tennessee State University.

Recent Titles in
Culture and Customs of Africa

Culture and Customs of the Congo
Tshilemalema Mukenge

Culture and Customs of Ghana
Steven J. Salm and Toyin Falola

Culture and Customs of Egypt
Molefi Kete Asante

Culture and Customs of Zimbabwe
Oyekan Owomoyela

Culture and Customs of Kenya
Neal Sobania

Culture and Customs of South Africa
Funso Afolayan

Culture and Customs of Cameroon
John Mukum Mbaku

Culture and Customs of Morocco
Raphael Chijioke Njoku

Culture and Customs of Botswana
James Denbow and Phenyo C. Thebe

Culture and Customs of Liberia
Ayodeji Oladimeji Olukoju

Culture and Customs of Uganda
Kefa M. Otiso

Culture and Customs of the Central African Republic
Jacqueline Woodfork

Culture and Customs of Zambia
Scott D. Taylor